"During my professional career I nev[...]
me. The San Diego Padres were m[...]
lucky to have had good managers an[...]
taught and encouraged me to be the [...]ould be. For my
hitting technique, it was Jack. His book will do the same for you."
—OZZIE GUILLEN, MANAGER, CHICAGO WHITE SOX

"This book is so fundamentally sound that I would advise anyone
considering picking up a bat to read it first. Watching Jack work with
the Florida Marlins hitters has proven to me how important a hitting coach can be."
—BOBBY COX, MANAGER, ATLANTA BRAVES

"Whether you are in Little League or pro ball, *Hit like a Big Leaguer*
will help you. It's excellent advice for anyone wanting to learn more
about hitting a baseball."
—ROBERTO ALOMAR, 12-TIME ALL-STAR

"Jack gives great advice. This book will help anyone develop their hitting ability. It can really make the difference."
—CLIFF FLOYD, NEW YORK METS, ALL-STAR

"As a young player with the Marlins, learning about hitting was very
important to me; and I learned a lot from Jack."
—EDGAR RENTERIA, ATLANTA BRAVES, FOUR-TIME ALL-STAR

"The techniques used in this book were instrumental in the development of my game. The drills and advice Jack offered me lifted my
game and took me to the next level. A must read."
—JEFF FRANCOEUR, ATLANTA BRAVES

Hit Like a
BIG LEAGUER

Hit Like a
BIG LEAGUER

Batting Tips, Techniques,
and Strategies for Coaches and Players

JACK MALOOF

McGraw-Hill

New York   Chicago   San Francisco   Lisbon   London   Madrid   Mexico City
Milan   New Delhi   San Juan   Seoul   Singapore   Sydney   Toronto

Library of Congress Cataloging-in-Publication Data

Maloof, Jack.
 Hit like a big leaguer : batting tips, techniques, and strategies for coaches and
players / Jack Maloof.
  p.   cm.
 Includes index.
 ISBN 0-07-146790-4 (alk. paper)
 1. Batting (Baseball)   I. Title.

 GV869.M425   2006
 796.357'26—dc22   2005024877

1 2 3 4 5 6 7 8 9 0   DOC/DOC   0 9 8 7 6

ISBN 0-07-146790-4

Interior design by Think Design Group
Interior photographs by Steven M. Terry

This book is printed on acid-free paper.

To Ben Hines

*During your many years in baseball,
at both the college and professional levels,
you have touched many lives.
Thanks for touching mine.*

Contents

Foreword

Playing for the San Diego Padres was a dream come true. After all those years of hard work, dedication, and accomplishments, the memories I walked away with were of my family, teammates, and those who were a part of my life during that very special time. Their devotion to me is something I will always treasure.

I met Jack during my first year in professional baseball, 1981, in Instructional League in Mesa. I was excited to have the opportunity to learn and further my development as a pro player. Although Jack's philosophy and instruction came early in my career, they helped confirm my hitting instincts.

In *Hit like a Big Leaguer*, Jack teaches the fundamentals he shared back then, with simple step-by-step instructions that provide solutions to the many challenges that today's hitters face. This book will make hitting a baseball fun and exciting and help hitters at any level of competition succeed.

Because I know Jack and his passion for teaching, it is easy for me to recommend this book to anyone willing to take the challenge and learn to "hit like a big leaguer."

Tony Gwynn
September 19, 2005

Preface

I have written *Hit like a Big Leaguer* to provide information for the amateur and professional player or anyone who is willing to learn more about the fundamentals of hitting. In today's society, education is the key to anyone's future. Becoming educated with the correct information can and will unlock a person's true potential to score and set him on the base path for success. *Hit like a Big Leaguer* was written and designed with those purposes in mind. It is my hope that the following pages will become a valuable source, complete with comprehensive information and pictures that will provide guidance, insight, and answers.

Although the mechanics of the swing are important and need to be correctly learned, adjusted, and maintained and consistently applied throughout a player's development and career, once a proper swing is achieved, I strongly believe that for the player to improve and attain the success he desires, his primary assets will ultimately be mental rather than physical. Prior to going to the plate and during his plate appearances, the level of confidence he has in his ability will ultimately determine the amount of success he will experience. Thus, how and what a player thinks and, more important, how much he believes in himself will routinely be revealed during his performance. Therefore, in addition to the physical and mechanical segment of *Hit like a Big Leaguer*, I have devoted the first part of the book to the importance of a hitter's mental approach—his attributes and overall mental perspective—as it applies to the game, his hitting ability, and, above all, himself.

Acknowledgments

I started thinking about writing this book more than 10 years ago, although the concepts and principles contained in it are something I've been working on for my entire professional career. A life lived in baseball is not always easy, but I'd like to specially thank those who have made *Hit like a Big Leaguer* possible:

Joan, my wife of nearly 37 years. We started out on this wild ride together, and I would not still be in the game if it weren't for her. Her love, devotion, and encouragement continue to amaze me. She has always been and will always be my partner in life. Thank you for being my number-one fan.

Justin and Jessica, my two children. A father could not be prouder than I am of you. Justin spent many hours working on the photos and captions for this book, based in part on his own personal knowledge and firsthand experience of the game. Thanks to his wife, Laura, for allowing those long editing sessions. Jessica has been working with words since before she started kindergarten and has read more books in 27 years than most people do in their entire lives. Because of that, combined with her professional editing experience, she whipped this book into shape and got it ready to submit for publication. Thanks for your love and support.

The Seibu Lions. Playing in Tokyo gave me an experience that most ballplayers don't get: the chance to see what it's like to play in an international setting. The fans were exceptionally supportive and knowledgeable about the game. The Lions gave me the motivation to pursue baseball as my lifelong career.

The San Diego Padres, Florida Marlins, and Atlanta Braves clubs. Each organization gave me the opportunity to teach in this exclusive area: hitting. Without those chances to learn and hone my craft, I would not be where I am today.

The players I've had the privilege of coaching over the years. Not only have I been able to teach each of them the best way I know how, but I've had the honor of watching many of them advance to the top of their game. Everything, from the 12-hour bus rides with no air-

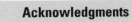
conditioning to the late-night curfew checks to the day-to-day grind of the long season to the championship wins and watching them grow both personally and professionally, has been exciting.

Dr. Garry Griffith, professional baseball broadcaster, teacher, and columnist. The persistence, encouragement, and many "red pens" resulted in this finished product.

Steven M. Terry. His time and professional photography skills were greatly appreciated. A lot of sweat went into making sure that each photo was exactly right. I certainly couldn't have done it with my own "point-and-shoot" skills.

Hit Like a
BIG LEAGUER

1
Positive Mental Characteristics

In my 30 years of working in professional baseball, I have had the opportunity to associate with many professional scouts. Their job is difficult as they evaluate players at all levels of competition. From high school and throughout the professional levels, players are rated, graded, ranked, and filed. Make no mistake, a hitter's tools are highly sought after and a major factor in what a scout looks for in a player. His size, physical strength, barrel speed, hand-eye coordination, power, and running speed are great yardsticks in measuring talent.

But there is another unseen quality that scouts look for and try to uncover. It is a hidden quality that needs to be highlighted and understood by every young hitter: the mental strength or toughness required to compete at the highest levels of play. A hitter's physical tools, although highly important, are only part of the total equation, which is why scouts have such a difficult task.

Over those same years I have also been fortunate to have been involved with many good, young professional hitters who have displayed their talent at both the minor- and major-league levels: hitters such as Tony Gwynn, Ozzie Guillen, Mark Kotsay, Roberto Alomar, Sandy Alomar Jr., Benito Santiago, John Kruk, Kevin McReynolds, Derrek Lee, Charles Johnson, Cliff Floyd, Jose Valentin, Carlos Baerga, Luis Castillo, Edgar Renteria, Preston Wilson, Kevin Millar, Randy Winn, Mike Redmond, and Mike Lowell. There have been others, as well, who have distinguished themselves and who over the years have proved themselves accomplished and dangerous hitters. However, like any hitter, they've experienced failure. They've experienced slumps and periods of adjustments. They have been fooled, swung at bad pitches, and made routine outs. What has separated them from countless others has been their innate desire to excel, to compete at a higher level than their competition, to learn from and minimize their mistakes, and to draw from within themselves a strength of character that cannot be measured—except over time and by success.

For a player, strong character traits such as dedication, trust, patience, sacrifice, responsibility, determination, and courage, combined with ample physical ability and an overwhelming desire to win, will be the tools that will lead him to his highest levels of competence. Building positive character attributes will help him develop mental strength and allow him to become more confident and aggressive in his overall hitting ability.

From a professional standpoint, here are some examples of positive mental characteristics consistently displayed by successful hitters:

- They *trust* their hitting ability. From an offensive standpoint, whatever the circumstance, situation, or final outcome of their plate appearances, their faith does not change in what they believe they can consistently accomplish.

- They display *confidence* in their hitting skills. Any adversity they encounter creates a challenge to learn and improve.
- They display a *willingness to lead*, either by word or example. They walk the talk of success with teammates on and off the field.
- They have mastered a *fearless approach* to succeed. They strive to excel with no limitations. For them success or failure is not a threat.
- They display a *patient, relaxed demeanor* during their plate appearances. They seem panic-resistant. They are confident in their present expectations and future potential.
- They display an *undying determination* to accomplish short- and long-range goals. They are dedicated to a consistent workout program and maintenance routine that prepares them for success.
- While at the plate, they respond *visually* to pitches, not emotionally to feelings.

As noted, accomplished hitters have developed strong mental capacities to coincide with their physical tools. In so doing, they have overcome many of the adversities that surround hitting. They have confidence in themselves and their ability, and that confidence has instilled a positive offensive mind-set. For those offensive-minded hitters, there is no doubt that aggressiveness is their underlying motive, and they show it. When they make a mistake, it usually is aggressive in nature.

2
A Mental Offensive Game Plan

Successful hitters have learned to hit by swinging, not taking pitches. For you, practice and experience will teach what pitches in what locations you can or cannot handle. Like accomplished hitters, as you develop you will learn to recognize your pitch and take advantage of it. You will learn to attack your pitch or capitalize on a pitcher's mistake.

Although strike-zone awareness, a hitter's contact zone, location, and count hitting will be discussed later, it is appropriate to mention another important reason why hitters succeed. Through experience, they have developed and applied the ability to channel their emotions and positive thought processes into a mental offensive game plan. For instance, in the dugout or while on deck, they have a definite purpose in mind. Confident in what they can do, they are determined to control their plate appearance, regardless of the pitcher's agenda. While going to the plate and relying on sound preparation and use of their strike zone as their guides, they are relaxed as their plan begins. Their concentration level intensifies, they are focused on early recognition of the pitch, and they are steadfast about what pitch (or particular pitches) they will hit and where they want the pitch in their zone.

Hitters who consistently get their pitch to hit, coupled with the avoidance of "bad pitches," are, in essence, dictating their plate appearance to the pitcher, catcher, and umpire. As a hitter that a pitcher must contend with, they are sending the message, "I know my limitations, and I'm in control." As a result of maintaining their mental game plan, they help ensure themselves better pitch selection, which will allow their mechanics to work more effectively and thus allow their tools to consistently surface.

Previously, I stated that a hitter's confidence in his ability will routinely be revealed during his plate appearances. While hitting, when you hear the command "Be ready!" what exactly does that mean to you? What it should signify is just that—be ready to swing the bat. Be ready to attack the ball with authority. To implement that process and offensive mental game plan, you should have a positive mindset and believe that pitch and, indeed, each pitch thereafter will be your pitch to hit. For example, as the pitcher is looking in for his sign and then begins his windup, a positive thought process for a hitter could be: "Yes, yes, yes" or "Hit, hit, hit." And then the hitter has a visual response to the pitch, followed by the action of swinging or not swinging, depending on its location. Confident, aggressive hitters are intent on hitting the ball solidly and are ready to swing until the ball says, "No, I'm a bad pitch." Conversely, negative or defensive thought processes question first: "Will it be a good pitch? Will it be my pitch, in my zone? What kind of pitch will it be? Are my hands in the right position? Will I get my front foot down? I hope it's my pitch;

I don't know!" Frequently the hitter's decision is not to swing but take the pitch. The call is "Strike!" These negative or defensive thought processes slow down your response time and disrupt your physical approach to the pitch. Usually, you will realize too late that it was your pitch to hit, and you'll end up fouling it off or taking it, regardless of its location.

A confident hitter first believes each pitch will be his to hit and then trusts his response according to that pitch. He displays the ability to recognize pitches early, make good pitch selection decisions, consistently time his swing on pitches he wants, and, as a result, show an overall sound mental and physical approach. As he strides to the plate and steps into the batter's box, he may be whispering to himself, "I believe the next pitch I see will be mine to hit, and I'm ready to respond!"

3
Fear

Even with the best of intentions, there are many reasons why successful hitting is such a difficult task to perform and many ways even the best of plans can be destroyed in a matter of minutes and open the door to adversity. Routinely, all it takes by a hitter is a mental shift of focus from his game plan to a pitcher's agenda, a lack of confidence or concentration, or the inability to control his emotions—all of which can put him in jeopardy of losing control of his plate appearance. Make no mistake, when mental lapses occur, all hitters at every level of competition face times when they wander into the real world of adversity. Outwardly, from mechanical breakdowns to bad ballpark lighting and backgrounds to facing a dominant pitcher or receiving an umpire's bad call, there are many situations and forms of distraction that are evident and could cause a hitter to lose his concentration, change his focus, or become overly emotional to the point of losing sight of his main purpose for that game or specific game plan. Subtly at first, adversity begins to surround a hitter who does not properly weigh the importance of his thoughts, his words, or the actions he takes concerning his circumstance. Often, a hitter finds himself in a slump without realizing why, and instead of making positive mental adjustments and relying on his offensive game plan, he changes mechanically and often finds himself in a deeper hole.

For every hitter, adversity will be a constant thorn and something to consistently overcome to be successful. In dealing with these problems, the hitter must first look inward and from a mental standpoint examine the unseen forces that are at work. Certainly, there are many other things that cause negative thoughts and emotions to surface and could be mentioned at this time; however, the one underlying menace that is out to destroy any hitter's best intentions and open the door to adversity is fear.

Fear is an overwhelming and potentially damaging emotion, and for a hitter it is at the root of defensive or negative thinking. It is an unpleasant feeling caused by the unknown or unexpected as well as by expectations of danger, personal pain, loss, or failure. Whether it's a fear of failure, fear of insignificance, fear of being hit by the ball, fear of getting beat inside or covering the outside corner, fear of mechanical breakdown, or any number of other unknown possibilities, for a hitter dominated by fear, any plate appearance can be fatal. There is no doubt that this emotion, fueled by feelings of insecurity, doubt, worry, anxiety, or confusion, can put him on an emotional roller coaster that is hard to get off.

Relenting to this damaging emotion with its negative feelings and poor thought processes, the questions, "Can I succeed?" "Will I react well?" "Can I hit this guy's fastball?" "Can I stay back?" "Can I be quick enough?" etc., can be devastating. While going to the plate, these negative questions, combined with the normal adrenaline rush of the moment, can cripple a hitter's real need to succeed. And it is at this critical time that if fear takes its hold, any hitter will feel its pressure.

It has been said that the only pressure there is on a hitter is the ~~pressure he puts on himself.~~ Needless to say, those hitters caught in ~~the jaws of doubt~~ or worry can become easy prey for any pressure ~~...~~ ability to consistently follow an offen- ~~...con~~trol their emotions, correctly channel ~~...~~ focus to become more visually aware

~~...~~ situation, a hitter who is worried or ~~...~~ the job done or getting a big hit or who ~~...~~ or overpowering fastball may feel the ~~...no~~rmally would or more than is actually ~~...~~ overreacts or retreats into a pattern ~~...t~~rusting himself and his physical abilities ~~...~~ preparation and offensive game plan, he ~~...~~ the moment and, from within, adds only ~~...~~ already electrifying atmosphere. Con- ~~...~~ shaken and he takes actions that display ~~...~~ muscled responses, coupled with defi- ~~...t~~aking wild swings that can be the result ~~...~~, he becomes tentative, slow, and usually ~~...~~ results in too many called strikes or ~~...~~ actions that are long, slow, and consis- ~~...~~ are indications that fear and its allies are ~~...~~ing is near.

~~...poi~~nts for you to use to combat any unwar- ~~...~~ you relax. First, either on deck or at the ~~...~~, trust and confidence are mental pillars ~~...~~ help encourage your body, the ability to ~~...~~ will help release a lot of built-up tension ~~...~~ demeanor during the heat of battle. The ~~...~~ easier it will be to control your emotions, ~~...~~ and focus on the job at hand. Ultimately, ~~...~~ earlier, and your overall response will be

~~...~~ I played many different kinds of games— ~~...~~ and Indians," hide-and-seek, tag, and mar- ~~...~~ I never wanted to go bankrupt, get shot, be found, get tagged, or lose a marble. But even though I did, I enjoyed just playing. As I grew older, organized games were available, from Little League baseball and Pop Warner football to Pony League and high school sports. The more I played, the more I enjoyed the thrill of competing—and the more I wanted to win. Losing left a bitter feeling, and I learned early that it was something I wanted to avoid. As each year passed, it seemed the crowds grew larger and the stakes to win increased. Whether it was a high school league championship game, a state playoff game, or a college World Series game, the goal to win continued to rise . . . and I enjoyed every minute of it. The higher the stakes, the greater the thrill!

It was during this time that I realized an important fact about myself and a second helpful hint for you. If I succeeded in doing what I wanted to do—and what I wanted to do was win—I helped the team. In fact, my desire to help the team win and succeed greatly exceeded any doubts or worries I might have had concerning my own ability to perform or what I could do wrong. Practicing and maintaining my swing was one thing, but the thrill of playing on a winning team was the challenge and the showcase I desired.

Although fear is real and its pressures will always be in the shadows, relying on sound hitting fundamentals while gaining confidence in yourself will help minimize its threats. However, to defeat this foe on a regular basis and set yourself on the right path to consistent success, your main strengths will be your positive mental qualities, your underlying attributes of toughness and aggression, and your overwhelming desire to compete and win.

4
Hit to Win

In sports, winning a game and defeating your opponent is deemed success. Games are played, and a final outcome is determined: one team wins, and the other is defeated. It's like playing marbles. However, at the higher levels of competitive sports, at the professional levels, and certainly at the major-league level, more is at stake than a few marbles. Over a short period of time, careers are on the line and millions of dollars are at stake. A highly successful team owner has been heard to say, "Just win, baby! Just win!" Yes, winning is everything, especially at the top of the competitive scale.

From my earliest memories, the reason I enjoyed baseball was the unique challenge of the one-on-one confrontation

between the hitter and pitcher. For me, wanting to win a game was always important; however, wanting to beat the pitcher was the game within the game. It was in that game that I wanted to hit to win. Like all hitters, I wanted to get a hit, drive in a run, hit the ball hard, get on base, score runs, and, as a result, beat the pitcher. As you have begun to understand, for any positive results to take place, especially on a consistent basis, a hitter cannot become defeated by negative thoughts or a defensive mental approach before he ever steps into the box. In any situation, being intimidated by a pitcher because of what a hitter sees may disrupt the flow of his offensive approach and as a result open the door to adversity and possible early defeat. For example, a hitter who is about to face a pitcher with an overpowering fastball or sharp-breaking curveball or both may waver mentally as he thinks to himself, "There's no way I can hit this guy!" For him, chances are good that he is staring failure in the face, and he will not be able to hit to win.

Here are other examples of situations that could develop fearful or negative thoughts, destroying a hitter's positive mental approach, his game plan, and his best intentions of hitting to win before he ever goes to the plate:

- Playing in front of a large crowd
- Being in a championship game
- Poor weather conditions—wind, rain, heat, cold
- Poor field conditions—lights, background, batter's box
- Poor or inconsistent umpiring
- A previous unsuccessful plate appearance

As I have mentioned, overcoming fearful, negative thoughts is a tremendous step toward success and should be the first step in hitting to win. Understanding the extreme importance of a strong mental approach that will coincide with your tools can, on a regular basis, lead to success. Conversely, a fearful, negative attitude can lead to failure. When a hitter finds himself in an adverse situation, a slump, or an intimidating circumstance (bases loaded, bottom of the ninth, tie score, etc.), how much he believes in himself and his hitting ability will usually determine how much success he will achieve. While hitting, an attitude of toughness needs to permeate a hitter's demeanor and join his other positive characteristics. Attitudes that reinforce positive winning results are depicted in the table below. This chart also gives an opposing negative side and its ultimate losing results.

Hitter's Attitude and Mental Toughness Chart

Successful, winning attitudes create strong mental traits—positive results	Defeated, losing attitudes create weak mental traits—negative results
Hitter makes no excuses for his actions or final results. He takes the responsibility for his plate appearances. He takes advantage of the challenges and opportunities that are given him.	Hitter makes excuses for his actions or final results. He shifts blame to others: umpires, opposing pitcher, field conditions, etc.
Hitter's desire to improve and succeed allows him consistent, quality work habits.	Hitter lacks desire to improve and has inconsistent or poor work habits.
Hitter is coachable and is open to instruction. He retains information and slowly begins to apply it during practice and game appearances.	Hitter is not open to instruction. He does not listen well and does not retain or apply information. He continues to make the same mistakes during practice sessions and game appearances.
Hitter is locked in mentally and physically during plate appearances. He is relaxed and visually enhanced.	Hitter is locked up mentally and physically during plate appearances. He is unsure of himself, physically tense, and visually impaired.
Hitter displays confidence and patience while at the plate. He is offensive-minded and ready to swing until the ball says, "No!" He consistently gets a good ball to hit and hits it well.	Hitter questions his ability and worries about what the pitcher might throw. He is defensive-minded, tentative, overly anxious, or overly aggressive and feels the need to overcompensate. He consistently swings at a pitcher's pitch.
Hitter displays an abundance of self-esteem and consistently is determined to beat the pitcher and help his team win. His desire to win exceeds any fear.	Hitter has limited self-esteem or confidence in his hitting ability. He displays an inconsistent mental approach, and overall his physical mechanics break down.

It is no mystery that winning teams have winning, successful players. Players who have talent and understand what it takes, on a consistent basis, win the small battles within each game, thereby securing the victory and defeating their opponent. Before and during each game, they have a high level of confidence, display a focused determination, and meet and overcome the challenge by their opponent.

Mature, successful hitters have learned to combine their strong mental characteristics with their exceptional physical tools and to use all to their advantage. They realize that to gain consistent, rewarding success and to overcome the adversity that surrounds them, they must trust in themselves, their hitting ability, and their desire to perform well and compete to win. This is the foundation they have established and have come to rely on.

5
The Frontside-Backside Approach

Before I begin this segment regarding the physical or mechanical approach to hitting, it is important to first introduce and explain the concept that underlies the entire approach. To begin, an illustration can be used of a hitter in his normal stance position. In the stance position, a vertical line can be drawn from the top of his head, through his midsection, and directly downward to a point on the ground. For a hitter, the vertical line represents two critical factors in understanding and applying this concept. First, it will represent his center of gravity, where his balance point rests. Second, it will represent the distinction between the two sides of his body and the functions they perform.

By dissecting a hitter's body in half lengthwise, the side that is toward the pitcher, which includes the front (stride) foot, leg, hip, shoulder, arm, and bottom hand, will be termed *frontside*. Conversely, the side that is toward the catcher, which includes the back (pivot) foot, leg, hip, shoulder, arm, and top hand, will be termed *backside*.

The concept: frontside-backside approach

The concept is that the frontside of a hitter's body (including the hands) will "set up" for the swing and mainly determine direction. While setting up for the swing, it will dictate body alignment initially in the hitter's stance and at the completion of his stride. It will help in stabilizing the hitter's body, particularly his lower half (from the waist down), for proper balance and weight transfer during the swing. It will also determine the direction, or path, his hands will take to the ball. Another key fact for a hitter to understand is that, on a regular basis, whatever directional action is taken by the frontside (including his hands), his backside will automatically follow.

Frontside determines setup, alignment, and direction.

The backside of a hitter's body, specifically his pivot foot, back hip, and shoulder, along with his hands, will be used to time and deliver the actual swing. As his frontside completes its function of setting up and stabilizing his body, a hitter's backside, along with his hands, can then deliver the actual swing action. To allow this backside timing and delivery of the swing, once his front foot has landed, a combined, simultaneous effort is simply initiated by a hitter's hands and back foot. To implement this initial action, when a hitter feels his hands start forward from their trigger or load position, his back foot simultaneously begins its pivot, or rotating, action. This pivoting action by his back foot, timed with the forward action of his hands, will set two critical factors in motion in the hitter's (backside) lower and upper halves. First, it will release a simultaneous inward rotating action of his back hip and shoulder. Second, it will start an effective weight transfer forward. The backside delivery of the swing will create the necessary quickness to generate the desired barrel speed for strength and power every hitter wants at the moment of contact.

Front-foot setup   Backside timing and delivery of swing

In learning the basic fundamentals discussed in *Hit like a Big Leaguer*, understanding and applying this concept should become a top priority. Correctly used, the frontside of the body determines direction as it sets up for the swing. As it does, it allows for the correct use of the backside of the body (along with the hands) to effectively deliver the swing.

6
The Hitter's Feet

The mechanics that are discussed in *Hit like a Big Leaguer* are within the concept of frontside direction and backside deliverance of the swing, and they revolve around four key fundamentals that all good hitters display while at the plate:

- Balance
- Direction
- Quickness
- Vision

In addition to their physical attributes and their mental approach, successful hitters have been able to achieve consistent success in these four areas. They have acquired, through hard work and experience, a solid foundation built on balance for good direction to the ball and barrel coverage of home plate, exceptional hand quickness during their swing, and a focused visional awareness of each pitch.

For a hitter to establish and display a consistent, explosive swing, the lower half of his body (from the waist down) must be addressed. The lower half can be viewed as a solid foundation that is based, primarily, on balance. For a hitter, the ability to achieve and maintain balance in his stance, setup, and swing will be the beginning point for the effective use of his hands during his swing to deliver a decisive blow. In the lower half, a hitter's feet, legs, and hips play a vital role in this process. Initially, they will determine proper weight distribution in his stance, correct direction and stabilization during his stride or setup, and effectively time the release of back-hip rotation and weight transfer during his swing.

To help you implement this information, beginning at a hitter's feet and moving up his body, I will explain each function much as I would if I were instructing a major-league hitter or a hitter at the high school level.

For good balance in his stance, a hitter should feel his body weight distributed over the inner balls of his feet, with the backside of his body, and certainly his lower half, receiving more weight than his frontside. An adequate weight distribution ratio, in his lower half, would be 60 percent backside to 40 percent frontside. He should never feel substantial weight on or over his heels or toes. However, if he does, he should turn his feet more inward than outward, with the big toe of each foot pointing toward the opposite batter's box. With slight bending at his knees, the weight should now be dispersed over the inner balls of his feet.

As he positions himself in his stance, he should have the inner half of his feet wider than the outside width of his shoulders, thus giving a more triangular shape, or look, to his stance position. This triangular shape should be maintained throughout the entire approach and finish of the swing to help ensure good balance on a regular basis.

Weight distribution ratio: lower half

Triangular shape: from stance through contact

7

The Hitter's Front Foot

For a hitter, his front foot or "stride foot" is a solution for efficient body alignment and stabilization and can either help or destroy his ability to effectively swing the bat. How a hitter uses this foot could well be the single most problematic area he encounters as he strives to successfully swing the bat. If he uses his front foot incorrectly during his approach and swing, a hitter will find himself off-balance, locked up rotationally, or flying open, and he will consequently make the effective use of his hands and the correct delivery of his swing virtually nonproductive.

Ideally, in any stance position—open, straightaway, or closed—a hitter's front foot, used properly, has three main functions:

- It strides or sets up the lower frontside half of the body.
- It correctly aligns the body, directionally, back toward the pitcher's mound during the setup and swing.
- It holds, braces, or stabilizes the front leg (and body) for a firm frontside during the weight transfer and swing.

To help control these three main functions for the correct use of the front foot, maintaining a stride length or setup of approximately four to six inches should be another priority. While setting up directionally, a short stride will easily allow a hitter to land on the inner ball of his front foot and use it to brace or stabilize his body for a firm frontside during rotation and weight transfer of his swing. Maintaining the correct use of his front foot will create good balance and put a hitter on the right path for an effective swing.

However, a longer step, lunge, dive, or any violent rush forward with this foot stemming from a hitter's eagerness to hit will take him off-balance moving forward and start a chain reaction of ineffective motions that are doomed from the very beginning. For example, an overly aggressive stride can cause the hips to drift or slide too far forward, resulting in a rushed, premature weight transfer that consistently travels to the outer half and heel of the front foot and ends on the outer half of the front leg and hip. Consequently, with his front hip now commanding this early transferred weight, he will use it to initiate hip rotation as his swing begins, causing his frontside to prematurely rotate away from home plate and consistently "fly off" the ball.

Another important reason why the front foot can be such a problem area and why a hitter should make a short stride length a priority is that, during the entire approach, a hitter's front foot tends to cover more distance than any part of his body other than his hands. Covering distance takes time. From a purely mechanical standpoint, no hitter will swing the bat with his front foot still in the air. Try it. It does not work. That is because the actual action of the swing itself will not take place until the front foot is on the ground. Whether a hitter's stride is straightaway, inward, outward, or upward, how much distance his front foot covers and the time it takes to land on the

Front foot strides toward setup position.

Front foot aligns body directionally.

Front foot stabilizes front leg and body.

Correct weight transfer to firm frontside

Premature frontside rotation—"pulling off"

ground before he can actually start the action of his swing is the critical point to understand.

A hitter whose stride is too long in any one direction consumes too much "air time," causing him, on a regular basis, to be late in his physical response to the pitch and, thus, too slow with his hands and delivery of his swing. This common tendency leads to other mechanical problems that are easily seen. A few examples are muscled arm swings that drag or lift the hands and barrel, a premature weight transfer with legs that do not function properly and that allow hips to drift or slide forward as the front foot takes its stride, and very limited service of a balanced lower-half foundation.

The reverse would be true for a hitter whose stride, or setup, is short (four to six inches) and has minimal air time. Landing early, or sooner, will allow a hitter's frontside to establish itself as well as give a hitter the desired time needed to physically respond once the decision is made to swing. It will allow for the effective use of his hands and entire backside to deliver the swing, with better assurance of good quickness and a balanced foundation.

In regard to time and distance and as a practical application for the correct use of his front foot and the action it takes, a good rule for a hitter to understand and follow is this: long, out-of-control strides will lead to late or slow hands during the swing. The longer it takes for the front foot to get down and establish itself, the longer a hitter has to wait before he can start the actual action of his swing. Short, controlled strides will lead to quick hands and barrel speed during the swing. The sooner the front foot gets down and establishes itself, the more effective a hitter's balance, direction, quickness, and vision will be. A good reminder is, "Long down below, slow up top. Short down below, quick up top."

As you are learning, time is critical. Time is involved during recognition and tracking of the pitch, the stride/setup for the swing, and the actual swing. In an article written by Paul Recer of the Associated Press entitled "Physicist: Hitting Fastball 'Clearly Impossible,'" (February 19, 2000)* it was stated that, "A batter facing a 90 mph fastball has less than a quarter of a second to see the pitch, judge its speed and location, decide what to do, then start to swing." In the article, Recer interviews Robert K. Adair, a Yale physicist who has studied the science of baseball. Recer states that Adair reported on his analysis of the art of hitting big-league pitching at the American Association for the Advancement of Science. Adair stated, "When Big League pitcher Randy Johnson throws a 90 mph fastball, it takes only 400 milliseconds—400 one-thousandths of a second—for the ball to reach the plate. It takes about 100 milliseconds for the eye of the batter to see the ball and send the image to the brain. It takes 75 more milliseconds for the brain to process the information and gauge the speed and location of the pitch. During those fractional seconds, the ball has already traveled 14 feet. The batter then must decide, in just 25 milliseconds, whether to swing or let the ball go by. If the decision is to swing, the batter's brain then picks a swing pattern—high, low, inside, outside. This takes 100 milliseconds. By the time the batter is ready to start his swing, 225 milliseconds have passed and the ball now is only 25 feet from the plate."

Adair added, "The swing starts when the brain sends signals to the legs to start the batter's stride forward. It takes 15 milliseconds for the fastest signal to reach the lowest muscle in the leg. The swing itself takes 150 milliseconds, so if the bat is to meet the ball, the swing must begin just 250 milliseconds after the ball left the pitcher's hand."

Recer wrote that Adair said, "The swing involves moving a two-pound bat at more than 80 mph and delivering as much as nine horsepower of energy to the ball. During the first 50 milliseconds of the swing, the batter can stop the swing and let the ball pass. But after 100 milliseconds, the bat is moving at 70% of its final speed and the swing can no longer be checked. Too much energy is moving forward, and there's simply not enough time for the muscles to react."

Recer continues, "The physicist said the batter not only must gauge where to put the bat but also precisely time the swing so that the baseball and bat arrive at the same place, at the same time."

Having instructed many players over the years, I have found a misconception on their part directly related to their front foot, the element of time, and the timing and delivery of their swing. As previously stated, the allotted time given a hitter for the responses he must make both visually and physically once the ball is released by the pitcher is critical. However, a hitter's misconception (or misunderstanding), and therefore their problem, lies not in the allotted time given a hitter for his responses, although relevant, but rather in how he uses that time to set up for the timing of his swing.

Within the concept of frontside direction and setup and backside deliverance, a distinction has been made between a hitter's frontside and backside actions. The frontside denotes direction, because it sets up to stabilize the body for the backside (and hands) to time and deliver the swing.

However, a major problem many hitters have concerning the element of time and their ability to correctly time their swing is they lack confidence or understanding in three key areas:

- Early visual recognition of the pitch
- Allowing the ball to travel longer in flight
- Their swing's quickness

Thus, they are confused: while hitting, they feel they do not have enough allotted time, and therefore they end up timing the swing with their hands and front foot, which sets in motion a deliverance of the swing by their frontside. An example of this approach would be a lunging front foot that creates a rushed weight transfer forward resulting in slow, muscled uppercuts with limited back-hip rotation and premature front-hip rotation that forces a hitter to rotate off the ball, or "fly off" the pitch. With this misguided approach, there is little regard to an effective front-foot setup, well-timed back-hip rotation, and weight transfer with the hands, which will help produce the desired quickness and strength ideally furnished by a backside deliverance of the swing. A hitter using his frontside to deliver his swing is, in essence, attacking the pitch with the wrong side of his body and therefore severely diminishing the correct timing and deliverance of the swing.

A hitter who is caught in this dilemma must first believe there is enough alloted time to properly execute his swing; otherwise, there would be no successful hitters in the game. Second, he must realize the difference between the time afforded him and the actual timing of his swing, and he must understand how the concept of frontside direction/setup with backside deliverance can help in this regard. To coincide with the concept, and as a practical guide, a hitter should view time as it relates to the frontside and its approach, while timing of the swing should be viewed as it relates to the backside and its actions: time = frontside/timing = backside. Both are important. Both are intertwined. Both need to work together, and, yet, both are different and can cause major problems when not correctly applied.

A front foot that is correctly used will land and stabilize early, affording a hitter the time needed to set up, recognize the pitch, and gauge where to put the bat, once the decision to swing is made. If the response to swing is "yes," then a hitter can precisely time his swing so that the baseball and bat arrive at the same place and at the same time.

For a hitter, regardless of his stance, the most consistent direction he can take to ensure good balance, body alignment and stabilization, weight transfer, free (inward) back-hip rotation, and barrel coverage of the plate is when the front foot lands early, against its inner half, while setting up toward the pitcher's mound. A short, controlled stride will consistently establish this action. To personally check for good direction by the front foot, a hitter can use this procedure: once the front foot lands with its toe pointed more inward than outward to ensure a closed front hip, he should hold this completed stride

Correct directional line back toward the
pitcher's mound

position, and a directional line can be drawn on the ground. The
directional line should run from the hitter's back toe through his
front toe and continue out toward the pitcher's mound.

Here are two common examples associated with incorrect front-
foot direction and the consequence when the stride is not toward the
pitcher's mound. The first example, referred to as "stepping in the
bucket," is characterized by a hitter who strides away from home
plate, toward the pull side of the diamond:

- Loss of correct body alignment, as frontside lands open
- Loss of consistent stabilization during setup
- Loss of balance during weight transfer and rotation
- Loss of firm frontside
- Loss of inward back-hip rotation, as front hip prematurely
  opens and rotates away from home plate
- Loss of backside delivery of the swing, as hitter pulls off the ball
  with frontside of body and hands
- Loss of consistent plate coverage with barrel of bat
- Loss of vision, as frontside delivers swing and pulls front arm,
  shoulder, and head off pitch

Incorrect directional line—"stepping in bucket": frontside hip and shoulder rotate away from home plate. Hitter experiences loss of plate coverage with barrel of bat. Hitter pulls off ball with front arm and shoulder.

The second example of incorrect front-foot direction, referred to as "diving in," is characterized by a stride direction that is too much toward home plate or the opposite field:

- Loss of free back-hip rotation as front leg "locks" during delivery of swing
- Loss of quickness in back hip and hands, as hitter uses primarily his upper half (shoulders and arms) to generate swing
- Loss of consistent hand direction and extension during delivery of swing

Incorrect directional line—"diving in": front leg locks, and hitter loses consistent hand direction.

A hitter who is having mechanical problems with his swing should first check his front foot, in the areas described, before making any upper-half or sweeping adjustments. It may take only a simple widening of his stance for better balance, direction, quickness, and timing to put him back on the right path for success.

8
The Hitter's Back Foot

For a hitter, the back foot or "pivot foot" is vital to an explosive swing. The back foot, because of its rotating action during the delivery of the swing, is the foot that initially begins a hitter's swing in the lower half of his body. Based on the correct functions of the front foot, a hitter's back foot becomes essential in timing with the hands, release of inward back-hip rotation, and weight transfer to a firm frontside during the delivery of the swing. It also serves as a positional guide to aid consistent plate coverage with the barrel of the bat.

The back foot, or pivot foot

To implement the timing of his hands with the release of back-hip rotation and weight transfer, as his front foot lands and he feels his hands start the swing forward, the hitter's back heel should begin to lift, allowing for a rotating or pivot action to take place on the ball of his back foot. This action ensures a timed release of (inward) back-hip rotation and weight transfer to help his hands generate the quickness, the strength, and ultimately the power desired at contact.

However, two common actions lead to problems when the back foot does not lift and pivot during its integrated and timed action with the hands during the delivery of the swing. The first action occurs when a hitter pushes forward off his back foot as the stride is taken, resulting in the following:

- Late hip rotation as a prior forward slide of the hips occurs
- A severe, rushed, forward weight shift, resulting in a loss of balance and stabilization by the front foot during the setup
- A loss of frontside stabilization, forcing the hitter to use his front hip and body (mainly his front arm and shoulder) to swing the bat
- A loss of inward back-hip rotation

The timed release of hands, back-hip rotation, and weight transfer

Back foot pushes forward during stride.

A second action occurs when, as the stride foot lands, a hitter does not rotate his back foot but "locks" it down or rotates late, during the swing. Common results are these:

- Swings that are over (or off) the back leg
- Improper, or loss of forward, weight shift, usually resulting in an uppercut during the swing
- Restricted, inward back-hip rotation
- Frontside and upper-half control of swing—specifically, the front hip, arm, and shoulder—usually displaying long, slow swings
- A loss of balance at completion of swing that carries a hitter away from home plate

To correct these mechanical problems by the back foot, a hitter can check his back foot in either scenario. If the problem lies in pushing off his back foot during the stride and before the actual swing begins, a hitter should check these results once his stride foot lands. Holding that completed stride position, he should do the following:

Locked back foot

- Check where the weight transfer has ended. Has the weight transferred and become distributed over or on the outer half of the front leg and hip?
- Check the upper-half body position. By looking down, are your eyes looking over your front leg or foot? Or is your head over your front leg?
- Check the back-foot position. How much has it moved forward from its original position? This is usually seen at the completion of the swing.

To correct this pushing action by his back foot, a hitter must start a turning or rotating action (pivot) on the ball of his foot at the moment his hands start the bat forward from their load (trigger) position. This action will begin and combine the timed release of inward back-hip and shoulder rotation and weight transfer with his hands during the backside deliverance of his swing while allowing for the existence of a firm frontside.

To correct a "locked" back foot, the same adjustment as mentioned earlier must be made by a hitter. In doing so, the same timed

Combined timed release of swing once stride foot lands: As hands begin to swing forward, hitter starts pivot action with back foot.

This action will begin and combine the timed release of inward back-hip and shoulder rotation and weight transfer with the hands during backside delivery of swing.

release of his back hip with his hands will be accomplished. The freedom for his back hip to easily rotate inward will be felt, as a consistent weight transfer to and against a firm frontside is completed.

The back foot is a positional guide to aid in consistent plate coverage for the barrel of the bat. Hitters are not all the same in regard to their physical abilities. Size, strength, speed, the bat they use, and their stance are some of the variables that come into play when dealing with proper plate coverage. To understand the importance of consistent plate coverage, a hitter should know how to determine the distance between his stance position and the plate in order to maximize his barrel coverage while gaining good extension with his hands during his swing. Maintaining good hand extension and plate coverage will eliminate the necessity to "dive in" or "reach out" for pitches on the outside corner, due to the fact that a hitter is too far off the plate or because he is too close—"step in the bucket" and "pull off" pitches. Once he understands this, when he steps into the batter's box, mindful of his body's position in relation to the plate, a hitter can confidently take his stride toward the pitcher's mound and release his swing, knowing he has the entire plate covered with the barrel of his bat.

Straight stance: back foot determines width between where hands will initially start and their relation to home plate.

Closed stance

Open stance

Regardless of the stance position a hitter uses—straight, closed, or open—on a consistent basis, his hands will rest (set) off his back chest and shoulder and over the area of his back foot. Instinctively tied together in this way, a hitter's back foot will automatically determine the distance (width) between where his hands will initially start and their relation to home plate as his swing begins.

For a hitter to implement consistent plate coverage during his swing, from his stance position and in sequence, he should bend slightly at his knees and waist, extend outward with his front (bottom) hand and arm, and comfortably tap the middle area of the plate with the end of his bat. Depending upon whether his bat end exceeds or falls short of this area, a hitter should make the necessary adjustment by moving his back foot farther away from or closer to the plate.

Adjustments will always be made during the course of a hitter's development and career, even at the major-league level. Although knowing how and why maintaining consistent plate coverage is important for his overall approach, and should be the norm, there are times during a game when moving slightly closer to or away from the plate may be necessary, depending upon what a pitcher is throwing and which side of the plate a pitcher is consistently trying to use.

However, another adjustment a hitter can make to cover the outside corner of home plate without compromising his swing's extension with pitches on the inner half or inside corner is to move forward or "up" in the batter's box, closer to the pitcher. By maintaining his original width from the plate, a hitter can move forward in the box and cut down the angle of the ball's flight to the outside corner of the plate and effectively cover the plate with the barrel of his bat.

For a hitter who believes he must be on top of the plate to cover pitches on the outer half, this adjustment will also relieve the anxious thoughts of, "I don't want to get beat inside; I have to get the barrel out!" By thinking these anxious thoughts, he then becomes susceptible to off-speed pitches. These batter's box adjustments are valuable lessons and will contribute to a hitter's success.

Determining plate coverage

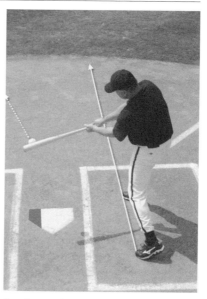

Consistent plate coverage—outer half of home plate

Consistent plate coverage—middle of home plate

Consistent plate coverage—inner half of home plate

Forward batter's box adjustment to cut down angle of ball's flight toward outer half of plate

9
The Hitter's Legs

The legs play an integral role for balance during a hitter's stance, setup, and weight transfer. They are also the area where a hitter's weight shift begins and ends in the lower half of the body during the swing.

For good balance in his stance, a hitter should spread his feet wider than his shoulders (creating a more triangular than rectangular shape to the legs) while slightly bending at his knees. In this position, a hitter should feel his body weight resting over the inner balls of his feet. He can then shift approximately 60 percent of his weight back over the inner ball of his back foot. In doing so, his weight should now rest along the entire length of his inner back-leg and thigh area. It should be noted during this process and the swing that, although bent, his back knee should not collapse its weight down onto his back foot and thus restrict its pivoting action.

Stance position—feet wider than shoulders

If his weight is correctly distributed as he begins his approach and swing, and if his feet do their appropriate jobs, a hitter's backside weight will stay back until the timed action of his back foot and hands release it during the delivery of his swing, clearing the way for an effective weight transfer.

A hitter who is having difficulty maintaining his balance throughout this process may have his legs too stiff or locked at either knee (or both), opening the door for problems to occur. In sequence, here are a few examples and consequences:

- Body weight is distributed toward the outside of the feet and on the heels, causing a hitter to become off-balance in the stance, approach, and swing.

- Back-foot pivot action is restricted, as foot tends to collapse inward or push forward (not rotate) during the approach and swing.
- Inward back-hip rotation is restricted, as hips slide forward during weight transfer.
- Inward back-hip rotation is restricted, causing limited barrel coverage on outer half of plate.
- Over time, a hitter may experience lower-back pain or serious injury due to lack of free back-hip rotation.

Body weight incorrectly distributed toward outside of feet and on heels

As previously noted, how a hitter uses his feet and legs in his stance, setup, and swing will determine the extent of balance, quickness, and strength he will achieve. This is extremely important to understand when dealing with weight transfer during the swing. A question that continually surfaces concerning a hitter's weight shift or transfer is where it begins and ends in the lower half of the body. It is important to remember that there is a center of gravity that runs directly down the middle of the body to an imaginary point on the ground. With proper weight distribution in his stance and the correct use of his feet and legs during the stride and swing, a hitter's weight transfer should stay as close as possible to his center of gravity. Assuming the previously mentioned factors arc understood, a quick review in sequence is appropriate to implement a consistent, well-timed weight transfer.

A consistent, well-timed weight transfer

As a hitter's stride foot lands against its inner ball, his back foot begins to lift and pivot, his hands start his bat forward, and the delivery of his swing begins. At the same instant, his back hip rotates inward, automatically releasing body weight, particularly in his back inner-thigh area, toward a firm (frontside) leg. As his back hip rotates, his front foot braces and front leg slightly stiffens to receive the transferred weight. The main recipient of the forward weight transfer now becomes his front inner thigh. During the backside delivery of his swing, and as his back hip rotates, a hitter's weight transfer goes from back inner thigh to against his front inner thigh. As this action is implemented, a hitter's center of gravity should maintain itself and not shift greatly from its origin. As a result, a hitter will maintain his balance throughout his weight transfer and swing, unleashing strength and power through the hips.

10
The Hitter's Hips

Good hip rotation is essential for a hitter; it is how he generates his strength and power during his swing. Following the concept of backside delivery, it is the proper release of inward back-hip rotation, timed with the release of his hands forward, that bring maximum benefit to a hitter's swing. To implement this initial action, the back foot and its pivot action will automatically start inward back-hip rotation and begin the weight transfer to and against a firm frontside. The critical point to understand is that by timing the release of body weight inward and forward, as his hands start forward, a hitter is using (rotating) weighted force to help drive his hands to and through the ball at contact. This

Proper release of inward back-hip rotation, timed with the hands and release of back-foot pivot action

Back foot releases inward back-hip rotation and weight transfer to inner foot, leg, and thigh.

unleashes the strength and power generated by his backside area and its delivery with his hands.

These are questions to ask or reference points to check during practice sessions for good (inward) back-hip rotation:

- Has initial pivot action by the back foot taken place?
- Has the stomach or belt buckle rotated approximately 90 degrees and finished facing the mound as the swing is completed?
- Has the back hip, during the delivery of the swing, rotated beneath the head?
- If balance has been lost, has rotated body weight (back hip) carried the hitter (inward) toward home plate as his swing is completed?

During the course of a hitter's development, the question may be asked: "As I swing the bat, what does the front hip do?" The important part to understand in the question is, "As I swing the bat . . ." As part of the frontside, once the front hip helps during setup and stabilization of the body, what it does or when it responds rotationally is totally dependent on when the hitter's back foot and hip begin their initial rotating actions and his swing begins. Throughout his swing, his front hip does virtually nothing but respond rotationally to what his back hip is initiating. With no emphasis on the front hip, its response to the back hip will be immediate and will therefore rotate freely, clearing the way for quickness, strength, and power during the swing. When a hitter does not establish correct front- and backside actions but instead uses the frontside of his body to dictate or deliver the swing, mechanical problems occur with end results being a loss of balance, direction, and vision.

Balance has to do with weight. The hips represent the largest area of muscle mass in a hitter's body, thus commanding much of his body weight. The amount of weight and how it is implemented will often dictate the emphasis of the action. Problems occur in the hip area when there is improper weight distribution during the setup or when, during transfer, the weight shifts prematurely to the front hip. For example, by receiving this (early) weight, the emphasis during rotation will automatically be on the front hip, and it will dictate the action for the hips during the swing. Because the front hip is part of the frontside and the frontside determines direction, not delivery, and because it now commands the weight, the emphasis during rotation will be on a directional path away from home plate and the ball, as the backside and hip automatically follow this outward direction.

When the front hip is controlling the weight during rotation, it can easily disrupt a hitter's ability to consistently achieve correct hand direction, extension, swing plane, barrel coverage, and head position. This large muscle mass rotates away from the plate, essentially "pulling" the body and the hands with it and away from the pitch. In the end, it will diminish inward back-hip rotation, the backside delivery of the swing, and finally a hitter's balance.

Front hip controlling hitter's weight during rotation

Before leaving this section on the hips, one important point needs to be emphasized. It concerns a common action taken by a hitter in regard to rotation, his front hip, and its use to generate hip rotation. It should be mentioned that successful results can be achieved. When the setup has been correctly accomplished and weight transfers when needed, solid contact can be made—but at a price a hitter may eventually regret.

Depending upon his physical strength, a hitter may have success by hitting the ball mainly to the pull side of the diamond, and with power. However, depending upon batter's box positioning and plate coverage, some existing problems will still remain and continue to surface:

- Inconsistent hand direction, extension, and barrel coverage of pitches on the outer half of plate
- Directionally rotating or "pulling off" pitches with the entire frontside of a hitter's body (hip, shoulder, and arm), causing restricted vision as his head turns and "flies off" the pitch
- Susceptibility to off-speed pitches
- A routine loss of balance

However, the critical reason to use the back hip to initiate and then generate rotation is to avoid the possibility of injury. When beginning rotation, if the front hip controls the emphasis, its force and weight as it rotates will dominate the effective use of the feet, the legs, and, in particular, the back foot. Instead, the back foot may lock down and inward, preventing or restricting its pivot action from occurring. This action will not allow the essential freedom by the back hip to rotate (inward) with the hands during the swing and therefore creates the problem. The rotating force and torque that is placed on the small of the back during rotation is tremendous, and without sufficient freedom for the back hip to easily rotate, it can cause lower-back stiffness or pain or a severe disk injury that may require surgery.

For a hitter to maintain quickness, strength, and power during his swing, and to eliminate the possibility of injury, free (inward) back-hip rotation is essential. While releasing the weight transfer, it should rotate naturally, beneath a hitter's head, while helping his hands deliver his swing.

11
The Hitter's Shoulders

This section focuses on the upper half of a hitter's body: his shoulders, arms, hands, head, and eyes. As with the lower half, each of these areas are linked together for maximum efficiency. Correctly combining the upper with the lower half of his body, within the concept of frontside direction and backside deliverance, will allow a hitter to implement a well-balanced, directed swing that displays quickness, strength, and power.

Mechanically, there will always be a reaction to an initial action taken, or a chain reaction to an action. When the initial action is correct, the right reactions that follow can allow for consistent success. However, when initial actions are incorrect, the reactions that follow tend to be wrong or inconsistent, usually with poor results. For a hitter, his shoulders, like the other areas of his body, are no exception to this rule.

In the upper half of the body, the shoulders and their surrounding areas (upper back and chest) are the second-largest muscle groups for a hitter. Like his hips, they command much of a hitter's body weight. Using and directing this weight correctly during rotation is essential. When properly used, the shoulders along with the hips can assist the hands with their rotating (weighted) force. Within the concept and during the delivery of the swing, the objective for a hitter is to combine the timing of these two large muscle groups—specifically, his back-hip and back-shoulder areas. As mentioned, to correctly time the action between back-hip rotation and the initial release of weight transfer, a hitter's (back-foot) pivot must begin as he feels the action of his hands start his bat forward and the swing begins. Correctly implemented, this timed action will automatically engage the back shoulder to rotate (inward) with the back hip, thus combining the two groups. The (inward) rotating force of these

Combined timing of the back-hip and shoulder areas

upper- and lower-half muscle groups will give the hands added quickness and strength during the swing.

As mentioned, during stride and setup, correct body alignment is established when a hitter's front foot takes a directional line back toward the pitcher's mound. In a straight stance position and setup, the front shoulder should be on a directional line back toward the pitcher's mound. With stances that are open or closed, the natural tendency is for the front shoulder to be aligned either toward the pull (open stance) or opposite-field (closed stance) side of the diamond. In either case, as the correct directional process takes place by the front foot, it will bring the front shoulder back in alignment with the pitcher's mound. This alignment should then be maintained as long as possible, until a hitter's backside and hands initiate the rotation process and swing. Once implemented, his front shoulder, like the front hip, naturally rotates away during the delivery of the swing.

Open stance   Closed stance   After stride

In a hitter's stance, during setup and delivery his shoulders should be as close as possible to a parallel plane with the ground. When used correctly, his shoulders can assist the arms and hands in maintaining a consistent level swing through contact.

During setup and delivery, shoulders should be as close as possible to a parallel plane with the ground.

These are some contributing actions that allow a level shoulder position:

- In the stance and during the loading action (trigger) by the hands, both elbows should be relaxed and in a downward position.
- To load the hands, the emphasis should be on the top hand in order to draw the bat back.
- To start the bat forward from the load position, the hands (not front elbow) should take a downward path toward the ball.

These initial actions will promote shoulders that maintain a more level position during rotation and generate the desired strength by the back shoulder during the swing, while assisting the hands through the ball at contact.

As noted, the front shoulder in conjunction with the front foot can assist the frontside in proper body alignment when it is directed back toward the pitcher's mound. However, a common problem can occur for a hitter if, in his stance or during his setup, his front shoulder turns or "coils" too much inward before delivery begins. From this coiled upper-half position, his front shoulder will have to sufficiently open to allow his hands to easily swing and extend to the ball, especially on pitches toward the center or outer half of the plate. As noted, when the frontside is directed correctly during the stance and setup, the front shoulder merely responds (rotates away) to what the hands and backside are doing during their timed delivery of the swing. However, for a hitter, it is the uncoiling action (or having to clear out of the way) of this large muscled area that can, as a result, disrupt the effective use of his hands during the swing. A common response by a hitter is to force (or pull) his front shoulder open during rotation or aggressively use it to help generate his swing. In either case, the chance for his front shoulder to respond easily and rotate away is lost, replaced by swings that are muscled or pulled off pitches.

Hitter pulls off pitch with front shoulder.

During the swing, the shoulders are the apex for the arms, wrists, and hands. Their actions are often related to how a hitter uses his arms during his stance and swing. As noted, shoulders that are used within the concept and maintain a more level position while hitting will contribute to consistent success.

12
The Hitter's Arms

While in his stance, a hitter's arms should be relaxed and in a downward position. Both arms should be bent at his elbows, creating an L shape for the front arm. His back elbow should be resting no higher than his back shoulder. During the stride, as his hands trigger the bat, his front elbow should maintain its L shape while his back elbow maintains its original height.

In the upper half of the body, during his swing and its initial phases, a hitter's hands should dictate the action. As his hands leave their load position and start their extended downward direction to the ball, his front elbow, from its L position, will begin to automatically hinge open. Simultaneously, as a natural action, his back elbow drops from its original position to almost against the hitter's backside, and as it does, the barrel of his bat drops below his hands as a natural barrel loop occurs. To counter this natural loop in the swing as the front elbow hinges, his back arm and hand should gain extension, allowing his back shoulder to provide strength during its (inward) rotation. These actions will give strength and quickness for his hands to bring the barrel back on plane with the ball at contact.

Relaxed, L-shaped, and downward-positioned elbows

During this critical phase in a hitter's swing, the position of his forearms and wrists is extremely important. As his hands and arms extend downward and bring the barrel on plane at the moment of contact, for maximum strength throughout his shoulders, arms, wrists, and hands, a V shape is formed, starting at the top of each shoulder, running the length of his arms and forearms, and ending in a strong position at his wrists and hands. This V position keeps his front arm (elbow) down and out of the way of his hands and wrists during his swing. At this position, during contact his wrists will hinge (break) at the base of each hand, producing exceptional barrel speed for quickness, strength, and power during his swing.

As the hands extend downward during the swing, the back elbow drops and the front elbow hinges. This action allows the hands to bring the barrel on plane with the ball.

V shape

During contact, wrists will hinge and break.

Barrel speed is accomplished.

As mentioned, how a hitter's shoulders respond during his swing will be directly related to what his arms do. While hitting, when his arms' initial positioning is incorrect or when they receive the emphasis to initiate the swing, problems lead to shoulders that tilt, lift, or pull out and away. The common results are slow, upward swings with barrels that drag under the ball, causing pop-ups, routine fly balls, or missed attempts; or the results are swings that pull off, taking the hitter and the barrel of his bat away from the ball. These routinely result in weak topped balls or attempts that are pulled foul or missed. Here are some reasons why:

- In his stance, a hitter has his back elbow higher than his back shoulder. As mentioned, the natural action of his back elbow is to drop downward against his backside as his hands initiate the swing. The higher his back elbow, the greater the drop. From this overtly high and extended position, a drastic drop will occur, tilting or dipping the back shoulder downward. The reaction during the swing will occur at a hitter's front elbow (arm), causing it to lift. From a tilted shoulder and high front-arm position, his hands and wrists will not reach the benefits of a V position. In response, their reaction will be upward, creating an O shape with the front elbow and arm, replacing the V position as the swing is attempted. Thus, a strong position is replaced by a weak one, and a poor result usually follows.

Back elbow is higher than back shoulder.

Drastic back-elbow drop causes front-elbow lift.

O shape with arms as lift in swing continues

- In his stance, a hitter has both elbows down and in a relaxed position, but during his stride, he triggers the bat by lifting his back elbow instead of using his hands. This action will cause the same reactions as stated previously.
- In his stance, a hitter has both elbows down but uses his front elbow (arm) to initiate the swing. Depending upon the hitter, this action can have three different reactions:
  - When the hitter's front elbow lifts, his front shoulder tilts upward, causing a reaction by his back shoulder to tilt (dip) downward. This intensifies the lifting action as his back elbow drops, causing the same results as stated previously.

- When his front elbow is pulled outward, it will prematurely open his front shoulder and cause his hands to "cut" across the chest during the swing, taking a hitter's barrel away from home plate; in doing so, his hands will lose their extension capabilities toward the inside of the ball.

To begin swing, front elbow lifts.

- When the hitter's front arm is used to trigger the bat and is pushed back to the load position by his bottom hand, it will extend back and stiffen. From this extended "barred" position, his front arm will initiate the swing, sweeping the barrel out and around the ball. Hand quickness and extension will be decreased.

In all three cases, these actions simultaneously engage the front shoulder, and thus the frontside, to dictate the delivery. As noted, these actions will disrupt the quick and effective downward use of the hands and a strong V position during the swing.

Within the concept of frontside direction and backside delivery, arm extension is important to understand and apply. The hands and back foot initiate the delivery of the swing. As the frontside sets up, the hands, in response to the pitch, extend on a downward path to the ball as (inward) backside rotation is accomplished, providing

To begin swing, front elbow is pulled outward.

Hands "cut" across chest; barrel is pulled away from home plate and pitch.

Front arm is used to trigger bat. Arm "bars," or stiffens, and will initiate a sweeping swing as proper extension and quickness decrease.

quickness and strength during the swing. The process for correct arm extension begins as the hands leave their load position at the top of the swing and start their downward extension toward the ball. In response, both forearms begin to extend automatically, as the hands go to the ball. For quickness and correct extension during this time, the emphasis should be on the hands, not the front arm or elbow. The front arm should be loose (not tight) to allow the elbow to hinge as the hands and wrists continue their downward extension. Simultaneously, the back elbow drops, as does the barrel, while both forearms and hands increase their extended path.

At this critical time, the (inward) rotating force of the back shoulder and arm gives strength to the hands, allowing them to bring the barrel back on plane with the ball. As the moment of contact approaches, a V position is reached, and at contact the wrists break, allowing the hands and wrists to deliver (pop) the barrel through the ball as contact is made. After contact and as both hands and forearms continue their extended path, the hands and wrists will automatically roll as they continue to extend the arms to full extension.

Correct arm extension starts with hands at top of swing.

Hands start downward extension toward ball; automatically both forearms begin to extend as front elbow hinges and back elbow drops.

Hands gain strength as barrel drops below hands.

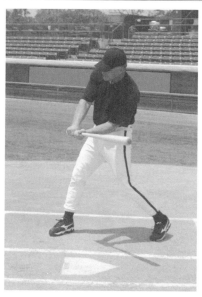

Hands bring barrel on plane with ball as V position is acquired.

V position—wrist break at contact

Barrel contact is made.

Wrists roll after contact.

During the initial stages of his swing, if a hitter emphasizes his front arm to gain extension (or full extension) prior to contact, it will stiffen, lose much of its hinging action, and pull his hands (bottom hand) forward during delivery. This pulling action by his front arm and shoulder will adversely affect his top hand and rotating backside strength during his swing, as his bottom hand virtually pulls his top hand off the bat, causing it to prematurely release after contact. Although deceleration of the swing begins after contact, this frontside delivery action will also increase barrel loop and drag, while decreasing hand quickness, strength, correct extension, and barrel speed before contact.

Premature hand release after contact

To gain full extension after contact and ensure the rotating force of his back shoulder during the swing, a hitter should maintain both hands on the bat until his back arm fully extends and after his wrists roll. During practice sessions, to build strength, muscle memory, and quickness, a hitter should keep both hands on the bat as long as possible while gaining back-arm extension, especially if the consistent results are missed attempts, pop-ups, or lazy fly balls. After contact, gaining back-arm extension as both hands swing through the ball at contact will automatically extend the hitter's front arm.

Both hands should remain on bat until back arm fully extends and after wrists roll.

Late bottom-hand release | Both hands on follow-through

While discussing extension, it is appropriate to answer questions concerning where solid contact is made. Questions include, "Why am I always topping the ball to the infield?" "Why am I consistently rolling over a good pitch to hit?" "Why do I routinely fly out to the opposite field?" Or, "Why am I not hitting the ball solid?" Answers involve early recognition of the pitch, the hitter's depth perception, his timing, and sound mechanics. However, other factors can be added that will offer more insight to these valid questions concerning contact. Although a hitter may have great tools, be mechanically sound, and have the desire to win, it is important to understand that how, where, and when solid contact is made is crucial for success. These issues will be discussed in the next chapter.

13

Barrel Angles, Swing Planes, and Contact Zone

While hitting, a hitter's contact zone, barrel angles, and swing planes change, which sends the ball to different directions on the field—fair or foul. Depending upon the direction his hands take at the top of his swing, a hitter's swing plane can be determined. The difference between a ball hit in the air and one hit on the ground is the plane that the barrel was on when contact was made. Because a hitter has a natural barrel loop during his swing, he must understand the importance of swinging with his hands on a downward plane and maintaining as level a swing as possible through the ball as contact is made.

During a game, when an attempt has missed, the odds are great that because of the loop of the barrel, the plane of the swing took the bat under the ball. On a regular basis, the number of missed swings, popped foul balls, pop-ups, and routine fly balls outnumber swings that are on plane with the pitch that produce line drives, hard ground balls, or balls driven in the air to the deepest parts of the park. As noted, when an attempt misses, the plane of the swing consistently takes the barrel under the ball. By realizing this, it is easy to understand why maintaining the correct downward action by the hands and arms to the ball and achieving a V position is so important.

Applying the correct swing plane for solid contact is one thing; applying correct barrel angles at the point of contact is another. Whether the ball is hit on the ground or in the air, the direction in which it is hit is determined by the angle of the barrel. During a swing, barrel angles are determined by when and where contact is made. As a pitch approaches a hitter, regardless of where the plate is, solid contacts are based in a zoned area (inward) from the front foot and depend upon where a hitter stands in the batter's box over the vicinity of home plate. This zoned area is within a width of 17 inches and a depth of approximately 12 inches. The 17 inches run diagonally from the inside to the outside corners of the plate. The approximate 12 inches start forward of the front foot to a depth just behind the front-foot area.

On a consistent basis, solid contact is accomplished within a hitter's strike zone and in this specific contact zone area. Correct V positions within the contact zone and barrel angles that produce solid contacts are based on an imaginary line drawn directly inward from the stride foot once it has landed.

Contact zone is based on stride foot.

Point of contact is ahead of front foot and contact line. Barrel angle is toward pull field.

In a V position, when the point of contact is ahead of the front foot and contact line, the barrel angle will be to the pull side of the diamond, and the ball will be hit early and pulled.

The farther ahead of the front foot that contact is made, the greater the barrel angle, and balls will be hooked fair or foul. However, during the swing, if contact is made too far ahead of the front foot after the V position and as the wrists roll, balls will be consistently topped on the ground to the pull side of the field. If not, the pitch is missed.

Point of contact is behind front foot and contact line. Barrel angle is toward opposite field.

Point of contact is made within contact zone and in alignment with front foot. Barrel angle is toward middle of field.

At the point of contact and within the hitter's contact zone, the longer the ball travels past the front foot and contact line, the greater the barrel angle will be toward the opposite field. When contact is made too late, balls are hit foul toward the opposite field side.

When balls are routinely hit in the air, popped up, or fouled off to the opposite field, the swing is too late for hands, wrists, and arms to recover the barrel from its downward arc and bring it back on plane with the pitch. As a result, the barrel drags as contact is made under the ball. If not, the pitch is missed.

When contact is made within a hitter's contact zone and in alignment with his front foot (on the contact line), the barrel angle is smaller. At that point of contact, a squared barrel angle (approximately 90 degrees) is made and balls are hit toward the middle of the diamond. The smaller the angle, the better opportunity for solid contact. Because a hitter's pitches are out over the center of home plate and because the most consistent use of solid barrel contact is at its more squared barrel angle, using the center of the field as part of his

Simulated contact zone and contact line based
on front-foot position

game plan and offensive attack will give a hitter the best opportunity
for solid contact.

During practice sessions, with the use of a batting tee and an
established contact zone and line as guides for his front foot, a hitter
can accomplish correct hand and arm extensions at a V position for
correct barrel angles at contact within his contact zone. Balls are routinely hit by recognizing and hitting pitches in predetermined pitch
locations within a hitter's contact zone to three main field directions—pull side, opposite field side, or up the middle of the diamond. Solid contacts can be successfully achieved.

For example, during a practice session, a hitter wants to hit balls
up the middle of the diamond. A batting tee should be used to simulate a pitch location that is over the middle of the plate. While a hitter is in his stance, he should establish his plate coverage and take his
stride. From where his stride foot lands, he should then draw a contact line on the ground inward toward the spindle of the tee. Regain-
ing his stance, the hitter can now set up and, as his stride foot lands

on the contact line, deliver his swing. If his mechanics, hand direction, and swing plane are correct and a V position was reached at contact, the barrel angle will automatically send the ball through the middle of the diamond.

However, on a hitter's next swing, if the ball is hit in another direction (pull side of the field, etc.), a different barrel angle will have been made. Seeing this result, a hitter will know, for example, that even though the ball was in his strike and contact zones, his hands took a wrong direction to the ball (sweep, etc.) and, consequently, he rolled over and topped it to the pull side of the diamond. This type of practice will give a hitter the practical understanding of when and where contact is made in relation to his body, swing, strike, and contact zones and how it feels to hit a ball solidly (or not) to a specific area on the field based on its pitch location.

Within the concept of frontside direction and backside delivery, here are examples of solid contacts to three main field areas, simulating pitches to three main locations of home plate. Each example is based within the contact zone and on where the stride foot lands in relation to the contact line for correct barrel angle on contact:

- Simulating a middle pitch location, when the stride foot lands on the contact line, a hitter can practice hitting the ball through the middle of the diamond.
- Simulating an inside pitch location, when the stride foot lands behind the contact line, a hitter can practice making contact ahead of his front foot and pull the ball.
- Simulating an outside pitch location, when the stride foot lands ahead of the contact line, a hitter can practice on a pitch that has traveled longer and past his front foot, hitting the ball the opposite way.

During a "live" situation, a challenge a hitter will always face in his quest for solid contact and success will be in his ability to recognize a pitch early, wait on the ball, and, once the decision to swing is made, be as quick as possible with his hands and delivery of his swing. The longer the ball is allowed to travel and the closer it gets to his front foot and contact zone, the quicker his hands must be dur-

Contact toward middle of diamond. Pitch
location is the middle of the plate, and
front foot is on contact line.

Contact toward pull field. Pitch location is
the inner half of the plate, and front foot is
behind contact line.

Contact toward opposite field. Pitch
location is the outer half of the plate, and
front foot is ahead of contact line.

ing his swing and the smaller the barrel angle will be on contact. The quicker his hands become, the shorter his swing will get, and as a result, he will develop strong V positions for solid contacts. Depending upon when contact is made in relation to his front foot, the barrel angle created will send the ball a specific direction on the field.

Although valid examples have been given to explain barrel angles and points of contact to predetermined pitch locations and to show how a hitter achieves solid contacts to those specific locations and fields, for every hitter the unpredictability of pitches and their locations in a live situation is the constant tangible fact he has to contend with during every plate appearance. However, this endeavor can be made easier when a hitter has, as part of his game plan, determined what types of pitches he wants to hit and where he wants those pitches to be, especially before two strikes. He should also realize, on a consistent basis, that hitter's pitches are ones that are left over the middle area of home plate, and he should anticipate that location for these reasons:

- It will help a hitter wait longer on a pitch.
- It will help a hitter respond easier to pitches on the inner or outer half of home plate.
- It will quicken response time if, initially, a hitter is looking too much outside or inside and then has to respond to a pitch on the opposing side of the plate. Usually his response will be too late.
- Although valid, it will keep a hitter from worrying that, "If a pitch is in, I have to pull it," or "If the pitch is away, I have to hit it to the opposite field."

Here is an example of a consistent mental approach to implement in a live situation. As a preliminary guide, before the ball is ever delivered, anticipate a pitch over the middle of the plate and *then* respond to the ball. As noted, using middle pitch locations and field perspective will allow a hitter to respond easier to inside strikes or pitches on the outer half of home plate, and when the pitch is over the middle area of the plate, the following examples will occur.

Assuming a hitter's mechanics are sound, based on a pitch location that is over the plate or down the middle, when a hitter is a little early in his response, solid contact will be made ahead of his front foot, and the barrel angle will automatically send the ball toward the pull side of the diamond. Based on the same pitch location, when a hitter responds correctly and makes contact in line with his front-foot area, solid contact will be made and the barrel angle will automatically send the ball toward the middle of the diamond. Again, based on the same pitch location, when a hitter is a little late in his response but makes contact just behind his front foot, solid contact will be made and the barrel angle will automatically send the ball to the opposite field. In all three examples of middle-pitch locations, balls can be driven to three different field areas, depending upon how long a hitter waits before he initiates his delivery and barrel contact is made. In each case, a hitter's swing will be short rather than long, and his bat's barrel angle at those points of contact will be smaller rather than greater.

For a hitter (apart from the known fact that his mechanics must be correctly learned, maintained, and applied), understanding the importance of when, where, and how solid contact is achieved can be of tremendous value. As mentioned, in order to help establish correct swing planes and barrel angles within a hitter's contact zone, the use of a batting tee to simulate predetermined pitch locations and the use of a contact line as a guide for his front foot for correct points of contact are practical aids during practice. However, during a live situation, a player must realize the importance of and advantages in allowing the ball to travel farther before contact is made. Having confidence in his instincts and hitting ability will provide a hitter the ability to recognize a pitch early, wait and track it longer toward its location, and gain the aggressive and effective use of his hands and backside during the delivery of his swing.

14
The Hitter's Hands

A hitter's hands make his final assault to a pitch and should be thought of as an extension of his bat's barrel. Within the concept, how well a hitter uses his hands will determine the effectiveness of his swing, the result of contact, and ultimately his offensive success. While hitting, a player's balance is directly related to how consistently he uses his hands for good direction, quickness, strength, and barrel speed through contact. The better a hitter's balance, the better he will use his hands. The better his hands are during his swing, the more barrel speed he will create.

While hitting, swinging a bat that is too heavy may hinder a hitter's balance, overwhelm his hands, and encourage the use of his arms, large muscle groups, or frontside to deliver the swing. This results in swings that are muscled and slow, with barrels that routinely drag under the ball. Although the ideal length and weight of a bat are personal matters and a hitter may change bats depending on his circumstances (slump, etc.), a bat should feel comfortable in his hands. It should also be well balanced and one he can easily swing, providing quickness and barrel speed during timing of a pitch and delivery of his swing. However, even when a bat feels right, how a hitter grips it may determine his effectiveness.

A top priority for a hitter should be freeing his hands to work together, correctly and efficiently, while allowing his body to support their actions. Correctly gripping the bat will allow this process to begin. Regardless of the bat, a hitter should grip the handle in the fingers of each hand, specifically aligning the middle knuckles of his top fingers with the middle knuckles of his bottom fingers. In his stance, the pressure of his grip should be firm but relaxed in his fingers, rather than tight. While hitting, squeezing the handle too tightly will put added tension throughout his hands, wrists, and forearms, restricting their freedom and thus barrel speed. Instinctively during his swing, the hitter will tighten his fingers' hold on the handle, allowing their strength to control the barrel and its quick path to the ball.

The grip—in fingers, not palms

Here are some reasons why the bat should be held in the fingers rather than the palms of the hands during the stance, setup, and delivery of the swing:

• Gripping the handle in the fingers will provide strength for the hands. There is no inherent strength in the palms of the hands.

- Gripping the handle in the fingers will draw both elbows down and inward, for a more relaxed start position while in the stance.
- Gripping the handle in the fingers will draw the bottom wrist downward, unlocking it to easily hinge (break or pop) at the V position during contact.
- When the grip is in the palm or across the pad at the top of the palm (where most calluses develop), the tendency for the bottom wrist position is to be high and more on a level plane with its forearm. This high and locked front-wrist and forearm position will restrict hand direction, quickness, and extension to a V position; as a result, a hitter must initially

Grip in fingers draws both elbows and wrists downward.

Unlocked wrist at contact

force his hands downward through this high wrist position and "fight" the barrel during the swing and through contact.

Incorrect grip in palm or across pad

In stance—bottom wrist is high, flat with forearm.

Locked bottom wrist—hand quickness and barrel speed decrease.

Questions concerning starting or resting positions for the hands are numerous. "Should they be high, and how high?" "Should they be low, and how low?" "Should they be forward or back?" Although a hitter may experiment with the use of a different stance or move his hands to different areas to compensate for inconsistent results, he should be mindful that where his hands rest and eventually start will directly relate to his arms and their efficiency and will determine important factors concerning comfort, timing, quickness, direction, and extension. Here is an example of how a hitter can let his hands answer the question of where they should rest and start, while determining where they feel most comfortable in the stance. In doing so, they will also allow his arms to relax and will provide a consistent load position during setup for his swing.

To implement the starting position for his hands, from his stance, a hitter should slowly wave the bat forward, extending his hands and barrel on a downward plane, through the contact line, simulating a swing. During this back-and-forth motion, the spot where his hands return to (rest) before each forward wave begins will consistently determine where they are most comfortable in their starting position to load or trigger the bat. Routinely, this is an area five to seven inches off the back chest and shoulder and as close as possible to the trigger position. It also draws the elbows in and downward and into their bent and relaxed positions.

Resting start position for hands—five to seven inches off back chest area

From this resting position, as his front foot begins its stride during setup, a hitter should draw his hands back to load or trigger the bat. During this motion, a hitter may allow some of his body weight to shift back as well, but the action should be a short, natural motion or rhythm that allows his hands to gather back (load) to where his body's backside weight should be resting. As a result, when the decision to swing is made and delivery begins, a hitter can use his hands and effectively time their response with his back foot's pivot and its release of backside (hip and shoulder) rotation and weight transfer, providing his hands more quickness and strength to the ball.

To implement and allow his hands to load while maintaining a relaxed front wrist and arm (L positions), a hitter should emphasize drawing his hands back with his top hand while his bottom hand stays relaxed for the short ride back. Although other areas (front knee, front shoulder, back elbow) are used for this initial and essential action, a hitter who correctly triggers the bat with his hands will maintain (frontside) body alignment during his setup with shoulders that are level.

Related trigger or load with the top hands

Common problems occur when other areas of the body initiate the start of the swing or the hands do not load or trigger the bat correctly:

- Initially, the hands drift forward with the front foot as it strides to setup. As a result, body weight tends to drift forward and a premature weight transfer occurs. The reaction will be a frontside delivery response.
- Initially, the hands drop to trigger the bat. As a result, as delivery begins, this "hitching" action does not allow the hands consistent time to gather or draw back, but instead they are thrust forward and up during the swing. Hand quickness and strength will be limited, and weak contact will routinely be displayed.

- Initially, the bottom hand pushes the bat back to load, causing two distinct problems as delivery begins:
  - Stiff or barred front arm occurs, with common results displaying slow, sweeping swings that pull the front arm and hands forward. This causes the loss of hand quickness, direction, and extension. Routine contacts are topped ground balls or lazy fly balls, as bat barrels drag around or under pitches.
  - A "wrap" of the hitter's barrel occurs as it tilts downward (flattens) and becomes more parallel with the ground as it extends past the head position. As delivery begins, the distance and time it now has to travel before it reaches the contact zone is great, in comparison to when the bat and its barrel are held and maintained in a more upright position during the setup.
- Initially, the back elbow lifts to trigger the bat. As a reaction, the back shoulder tilts upward as the swing begins. The hands may move back; however, the high and now-active back elbow will descend rapidly against the body's backside and, as a result, will thrust the hands and frontside up during the swing. Common results are poor swing planes, uppercuts, balls in the air, or missed attempts.
- Initially, to trigger the bat, the front shoulder or knee coils inward. The hands may go back; however, the reaction to this coiling action will be an initial loss of body alignment, and as delivery and rotation begin, the frontside will prematurely open causing the front hip, elbow, or shoulder (or all three) to fly open during the swing. A loss of hand direction, plate coverage, and balance are common results.
- Initially, the hands rest and start from the middle chest area. As with the front foot and the length of its stride, covering distance takes time, and too much time disrupts timing of the swing. Too long of a trigger action uses time, and as a result the hands may not fully load but instead may be rushed to deliver the swing. Common results are late swings, barrels that drag, missed attempts, or weak contact.

- Initially, the hands rest and start at the back chest or shoulder area but are extended outward too far. At a distance of eight to ten inches from the back chest, the front arm will lose its relaxed and L-shaped position as tension (stiffness) is added in the front forearm. Drawing the hands in and back to start the loading action will use time; the more time is involved, the more precise the timing must be for solid contact.

Within the concept, it is important for a hitter to realize that although both hands need to work together, each hand has distinct roles that determine their overall performance. Understanding their specific functions will allow a hitter to effectively combine their effort and maximize their use.

15
The Hitter's Bottom Hand

The bottom hand is part of the frontside and thus determines hand direction and arc of the barrel during the swing. At the top of his swing, as a hitter starts his hands forward from their load position, whatever direction his bottom hand takes, his top hand will automatically follow. When leaving their load position, correct direction is taken by both hands when the bottom hand leads in a downward extended path toward the inside portion of the ball. In response to this initial action, the front elbow begins to hinge, the back elbow drops, and, as the shoulders rotate, both hands quickly gain arm extension to a V position. At contact, the bottom-hand wrist hinges and both hands "pop" the barrel through the ball and continue their full extension of the swing.

Poor barrel angles and swing planes are created when the timing of the swing is too early (well ahead of the front foot) or too late (well behind the front foot). However, even when a hitter's timing is adequate, poor barrel angles and planes are created when the bottom hand leaves the load position and takes the wrong direction to the ball. Here are some examples:

Projected hand direction

Hand extension toward inside portion of ball—all three fields are attached: center, opposite, and pull.

Bottom hand is pushed or reaches for pitch. Sweep swing occurs.

- The bottom hand extends (or is pushed) across the plate or reaches for a pitch down the middle or outer half of the plate. This initial action will cause a swing to sweep out and around the pitch and barrel contact to be on the outer portion of the ball. If the barrel is on plane, most results are topped ground balls (as the top hand smothers over a premature and fully extended bottom hand and arm) or balls that are pulled or hooked fair or foul. If the barrel drags under the ball on contact, most results are routine fly balls or pop-ups to any field, fair or foul, or, depending on the hitter, deep fly balls to the pull side of the diamond.
- The bottom hand cuts (or is pulled) inward across the chest, decreasing hand extension as the swing takes the barrel away from the ball. If the location of the pitch is on the outer half of the plate, regardless of the barrel's plane, most attempts are missed or contact is weak and off the end of the bat. If the location of the pitch is on the inner half of the plate (and because of decreased hand extension), barrel contact will be on the outer half of the ball. Common results are chopped ground balls to the pull side of the field, fair or foul.

Bottom hand "cuts" or is pulled inward across chest, decreasing hand extension as swing takes barrel away from ball.

- As delivery begins, the bottom hand swivels upward (or is lifted), causing an uppercut as the front elbow and shoulder tilt up during the swing. Common results are missed attempts, foul balls, pop-ups, or routine fly balls as long, slow swings are consistently under the ball.

The bottom hand also controls the arc of the barrel, and its natural tendency is to swing upward. Swing your bat with just your bottom hand. It should feel difficult to control the barrel's flight, from its high, overhead position to a plane that is on line or level with a pitch at contact, as it naturally arcs down and then upward, as the swing is completed. During a regular swing, if too much emphasis is placed on your bottom hand to deliver the swing, combined with the drop of your back elbow, the natural loop will become even more significant.

There are reasons why, when the arc dominates the path of the barrel, slow, upward, and long swings occur, displacing swings that provide ideal hand direction, quickness, strength, and a level plane at contact:

Bottom hand swivels upward, causing an uppercut.

Bottom hand controls the arc of the barrel and its natural tendency to swing upward.

- An overtly high back elbow, or one that lifts to trigger the hands, will descend rapidly and tilt the front elbow and shoulder (up) while dropping the back shoulder, overwhelming the hands (bottom hand) and their downward extended path.
- Initially, from the load position the front elbow lifts, causing an upward reaction by the hands and disrupting downward direction and extension.
- Initially, the bottom hand rotates (swivels) upward, causing the top hand to swivel under the bottom hand. At the top of the swing, as the barrel begins its loop, it will continue on its upward arc through the completion of the swing.

Here are examples to help a hitter's bottom hand compensate for this arc and natural barrel loop tendency:

- A hitter can think, "Keep my front elbow down and out of the way of my hands during the swing." To implement, when leaving the load position without forcing his front elbow down, a hitter should practice applying this process, feeling his hands gain downward direction, quickness, and extension without being impeded by a high front elbow.
- A hitter can think, "Keep the barrel above my hands during the swing," encouraging a downward plane to the ball without a chopping action.
- As a hitter grips his bat, his bottom hand is against or close to the knob of the bat. During his stance and stride, the knob should be positioned in a downward angle. When leaving the load position at the top of the swing, the bottom hand should be able to control the knob and keep it on a downward plane, as the hitter's hands extend toward the ball. When implemented, this will eliminate the initial swivel tendency of the bottom hand (and knob) to rotate up and allow both hands to extend downward toward the inside of the ball.
- As noted, gripping the handle in the fingers of the hitter's bottom hand will lower the front wrist and draw his front elbow down.

16
The Hitter's
Top Hand

The top hand is part of the backside and controls the plane of the barrel for a level swing while providing strength during delivery.

As was described with the bottom hand, a hitter should swing a bat with just his top hand. From your resting position, draw your top hand back to load, and then swing. It should be evident how easy it is for your top hand to control the flight of the barrel and swing it on a downward and more level plane, compared to your bottom hand. What makes the difference between the two and allows your top hand to easily

Top hand controls the plane of the barrel for a level swing.

level the plane of the barrel? The answer lies in the strength it acquires during inward rotation and transfer of weight by the two large muscle groups in your backside (hip and shoulder areas), compared to your bottom hand's strength during outward rotation by the two opposing muscle groups in your frontside.

During backside delivery of swing, the combined strength of two large muscle groups rotating inward helps the top hand bring the barrel back on plane with the ball and both hands deliver swing.

However, for your top hand and its acquired strength to effectively combat the natural loop of the barrel during the swing, it must rely on the efficiency of your bottom hand and its initial downward direction.

For example, once your decision to swing is made and your balance and timing are good, if the direction by your bottom hand, as it leaves the load position, takes a downward extended plane toward the inside portion of the ball, your top hand will follow and gain strength during (inward) rotation of the back shoulder and hip during weight transfer. This is such a critical time during the swing because before contact is made, the barrel, as it begins its descent and natural loop, will descend below and stay below your hands until the strength of your backside and top hand are able to bring it up and on plane with the ball. The initial downward (extended) action and direction by your bottom hand will allow your top hand and its acquired strength to offset the natural loop and help both hands

The initial downward extended plane of the bottom hand is toward the inside portion of the ball.

As the bat barrel begins its descent and natural loop, it will descend below the hands.

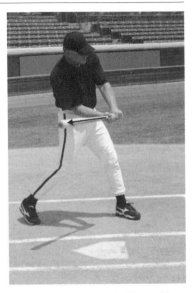

Inward rotating strength of backside and top hand are able to bring the barrel up and on plane with the ball.

bring the barrel back on plane and "pop" it through the ball at contact.

When a hitter has taken good direction with his bottom hand toward the ball and has combined that action with the strength of his backside and top hand to level and deliver the swing, hand quickness, strength, and barrel speed will be the result, with barrel angles and planes that produce consistent solid contact. However, if a frontside delivery is implemented and poor direction is taken by his bottom hand, his backside and top hand will obediently follow that direction. As a result, the hitter will lose balance, quickness, and strength, and contact will be inconsistent.

Within the physical concept, when balance, correct direction, and strength are provided by a player's body, his hands will effectively work together, and their assault to a pitch will be quick (short) and on plane with the ball. A relaxed grip within the fingers of both hands will add quickness and strength and allow them unrestricted freedom in their downward direction to and through the ball at contact. As a result, barrel speed, angles, planes, and swing extension will improve, as will solid contacts.

17
The Hitter's Head

Before getting into the chapters dealing with the head and eyes, it is important to realize that the concept described in this book and its physical approach have been designed to put a hitter's head and eyes in their best position to see the pitch. By maintaining balance, the effective use of frontside direction, weight transfer, and backside deliverance, a hitter will allow his head to remain still and his eyes to remain focused on seeing the pitch from the pitcher's release point to the hitter's point of contact.

As noted, there is significant body weight in a hitter's upper half. To control his upper-half weight for balance and to harmonize it with his lower half, a hitter should keep his head back and over his center of gravity during his stride and swing. As his front foot correctly sets up to stabilize his lower half and his hands start forward and down, by keeping his head position back and over his center (belt buckle), a hitter's upper-half weight (back-shoulder area) will stay back and simultaneously rotate forward with his lower half. During his swing, to maintain and practice this action, a hitter should feel his back hip and shoulder rotate beneath his head.

A hitter's head should stay still and calm. In his stance, any pronounced body movements, such as bending, bouncing, rocking, or jerking, should be done prior to a pitcher's windup. During the swing, any aggressive actions that cause the head to bounce, turn, raise, or tilt upward can cause loss of sight while tracking a pitch or just before contact. For example:

- A hard landing by the front foot may cause the head to bounce.
- A push forward off the back foot may cause the head to raise.
- A premature opening by the front hip or shoulder, during rotation, may cause the head to turn outward.
- A lift by the front elbow or shoulder may cause the head to tilt upward.
- A cutting direction by the hands, across the chest, as the front elbow pulls outward may cause the head to turn outward.
- A severe drop by a high back elbow may cause the head to tilt upward.
- A collapse by the back knee may cause the head to tilt upward.
- A severe bend at the waist may cause the head to rise during the swing.

Within the concept of backside delivery, another reason it is important for a hitter to swing on a downward plane is to allow his head and eyes to be in a downward position on the ball. To help maintain this position during contact, a hitter should try to follow the ball off his bat with his eyes. Even on a missed attempt, his head should be in a more downward than upward position and toward the direction from which the ball has come—the pitcher's mound.

However, when the hitter's head aggressively turns away or lifts during his swing and its completion, a frontside delivery has occurred, pulling his head and eyes off the pitch.

Head down, eyes on ball

Balance is a key component in a hitter's swing. Your head position will tell whether or not you are maintaining your balance over your center of gravity during your stride's setup and swing. These are two other common results of poor head position:

- As the swing is completed, head position is over or ahead of the front foot, well past the inner front thigh. These are a few reasons why this may occur:
  - During his stride, a hitter has pushed off his back foot, causing his head (and hips) to drift forward with his front foot. A premature weight transfer will develop, leaving him no choice but to deliver his swing with his frontside, thus putting him off-balance forward.
  - During his swing, a hitter pulls his hands forward with his front arm and elbow, causing weight in his upper half to drift and his head to lean forward.
  - As his front foot stabilizes his lower half and delivery begins, a hitter's upper half (front shoulder) and head drift forward

with his hands as they leave their load position. Frontside delivery actions occur (hip, shoulder, arm) that pull forward, outward, and up.

- As the swing is completed, head position is too far back or behind the back leg. Here are some reasons why this may occur:
  - To start his swing, an aggressive lift of his front elbow tilts his front shoulder up. As his swing continues, his upper half (weight) and head are rocked backward.
  - As his swing begins, his back foot locks down (does not pivot) and cannot easily initiate back-hip rotation and correct weight transfer forward against his front leg. As his swing continues, his upper-half body weight shifts his head backward, dropping his back shoulder and collapsing his back leg.

Common results of these actions are uppercuts, late and slow swings, missed attempts, pop-ups, or routine fly balls.

To maintain correct head position, when the hitter is in his stance, as he turns his head toward the pitcher, his chin should be on or near his front shoulder. In this position, his head should be resting over his body's center of gravity. During backside delivery, as his hands start their downward extended path and shoulder rotation begins, instinctively his front shoulder will leave his chin and begin to rotate away. Simultaneously, inward backside rotation begins, and as it continues, his back shoulder will rotate forward and automatically meet his resting head and chin as full extension is accomplished. Thus, to help maintain his balance while hitting, the correct head position should be chin near front shoulder from stance position to chin meeting back shoulder at full extension and completion of the swing.

To maintain head position, chin is near front shoulder in stance position and near back shoulder at completion of swing.

18
The Hitter's Eyes

A hitter's eyes hold a final key to his physical approach. Correctly learning, applying, adjusting, and maintaining mechanics will be a needed and constant process. Early recognition of a pitch and its rotation and location will be a hitter's greatest offensive challenge and should become his top priority. This physical concept, with its four basic fundamentals of balance, direction, quickness, and vision, was designed to put a hitter's head and eyes in their best position to see and judge a pitch early and then correctly respond. His ability to first process information visually and then correctly respond physically will determine his degree of success.

For a hitter to concentrate and become visually aware requires confidence in his hitting ability. As noted, confidence provides relaxation. The more relaxed a hitter is, the better he responds, physically and visually. His ability to correctly repeat responses and actions that are successful is the reward of a confident, relaxed, and visually aware hitter.

However, when a hitter loses his confidence, he loses his ability to relax, intensify his concentration, and visually respond well to a pitch. Like other areas of his body, his eyes are surrounded by muscles. When these muscles are tense or under stress, they will tighten and can restrict a hitter's ability to clearly see or focus. As a result, his judgment, decision making, and timing become inconsistent, causing mechanical problems in his swing to make it routinely rushed, forced, or late. Consequently, the first adjustment a hitter should make when his confidence begins to waver or any adversity surfaces is to relax, see the ball sooner, and stay on the ball longer. Then, he should make a mechanical adjustment if needed.

During plate appearances, a hitter's concentration level demands his complete focus on his main purposes: being offensive-minded (believing the next pitch will be his to hit) and seeing the ball from the pitcher's release point to contact. A hitter who worries about his mechanics (getting his front foot down or maintaining proper hand position, for example) while at the plate, gets upset by an umpire's bad call, or allows any other distraction to disrupt his swing, add to his tension, or divide his concentration will lose his ability to relax, recognize the pitch early, and respond correctly. Trying to adjust to two (let alone three or four) different things or pitches will severely affect a hitter's visual awareness and his ability to instinctively respond to what he sees.

Your eyes work like a camera. They can adjust and focus on objects far away or up close. When looking directly at an object, they sharply focus on the object; at the same instance, its surroundings become out of focus or dull. Try it. Look directly at any object, and notice that it is clear. Your eyes are in a sharp focus mode; by comparison, other objects, although visible and in your peripheral vision, are out of focus and dull. While hitting, what mode would you want your eyes in when picking up the ball from a pitcher, sharp or dull? I am sure your answer would be sharp. When you are hitting well, whether you realize it or not, your concentration level is high and undivided, you are relaxed, and your eyes are in a sharp focus mode. At a pitcher's release, they are able to recognize the pitch early, and while in flight the ball looks as big as a beach ball. As a result, you instinctively respond well.

To allow his eyes to be in sharp focus at a pitcher's release point, a hitter should ask: "In my stance, as the pitcher is looking in to get his sign from the catcher, what exactly are my eyes focused on?" It is an important question. Different explanations have been given. "They're on the pitcher—his entire body." "They're on the ball, either down at his side or in his glove." "They're on his upper half or on a specific shoulder."

During different stages of the windup, prior to the pitcher's release, where are the hitter eyes? What are they focused on? Most answers are the same, with an exception being, "At his release point." From one pitcher to the next, windups and release points change. If you are a hitter using any of these examples, your eyes, in their attempt to stay focused, are traveling from one area to another. You have "wandering eyes." For example, a pitcher who has a high leg kick or twirls his back to home plate, flips his glove out and up prior to release, or looks all arms and elbows ("herky-jerky") during his windup distracts the hitter's eyes and their ability to effectively focus at the time of his release.

Focusing your eyes at a pitcher's release point too early will cause them to automatically focus on something in the surrounding distance, and they will be out of focus at 60 feet. As a result, when a pitcher with good arm speed delivers the pitch, refocusing your eyes back to 60 feet for early recognition will be late. Consequently, so will your response.

As noted, when a hitter does not see a pitch early, his eyes have been distracted or are out of focus. Playing in ballparks with poor backgrounds, poor lighting, sun glares (off fences), or shadows could compound the problem, thus making the ball seem smaller or quicker or as if it is breaking harder. They leave a hitter wondering what happened during his failed plate appearance. After he has struck out, it is not uncommon to hear a hitter say, "I can't believe how tough that pitcher was; I never saw the ball!" or "With that windup, I never even saw the pitch, let alone hit it!" And it is true; without

Eyes focused too early on pitcher's release
point

properly giving your eyes the opportunity to clearly focus on the ball
at a pitcher's release point and track it during contact, even under
ideal conditions and with sound mechanics, successful results will be
inconsistent.

For your eyes to be correctly focused prior to the release point,
you should sharpen focus on a pitcher's head or hat. While doing so,
a pitcher's body and his particular windup, regardless of its motion,
will become peripheral or dull. A question may be asked, "Why
sharpen focus on a pitcher's head or hat?" Consistently, a pitcher's
head will remain steady and unobstructed during his windup and
will be in close proximity to his arm and hand as he releases the ball
(over the top, three-quarter, or sidearm). As he delivers the pitch, it
will be easy for your eyes to make the transition from a pitcher's head
to his release point.

During the pitcher's windup, focus eyes on the pitcher's head. As he delivers the pitch, flip eyes from the pitcher's head to his release point.

This simple process will train your eyes to not wander or become distracted or out of focus. A hitter can practice training his eyes to sharp focus at any time or any place; for example, he can practice as a passenger in a car or while watching TV. On the field, he can practice "flipping" his eyes each time he plays catch with a teammate and when taking batting practice.

There is a reason it is said that good hitters have good hand-eye coordination. Without the correct use of recognizing a pitch early, tracking its flight, and staying on the ball during contact, a hitter suffers the consequences of inconsistency and poor results. Make no mistake, your eyes play a major role in the success of your physical approach. They set the stage, prepare the way, and ultimately determine the degree and consistency of contact.

19
Strike Zone, Location, and Count Hitting

During practice, a hitter maintains his mechanics by repetitious action. A relaxed, acquired feel of specific motions and actions builds muscle memory into every phase of his approach and enables correct visual and physical responses to take place. However, during a game, a hitter must have confidence to rely on his practice sessions and physical approach so he can instinctively, automatically, and correctly respond to what his eyes see. While the hitter is at the plate, as the pitcher is looking in for his sign, the time for thinking about mechanics or feeling the motions and actions of his swing are over. It is now time to relax, recognize, and respond.

"Relax, recognize, and respond." Easy to say, but difficult to apply. However, a hitter who has a mental game plan and has learned to maintain and trust his physical approach can make that process easier and take another significant step toward offensive success by knowing his personal strike zone. While at the plate, a hitter who has a mental awareness of his strike zone will consistently get his pitch to hit and, as a result, maintain his mechanics and produce more solid contact.

Personal strike zone

For a hitter, understanding and using his strike zone will lead to quality swings. Quality swings will lead to quality plate appearances. Quality plate appearances will lead to quality offensive games. The more quality offensive games a hitter can display, the more he will have earned the title "dangerous hitter." In contrast, a hitter who does not have a mental game plan, does not know his strike zone, and has no mental picture of where he wants the pitch will consistently chase bad pitches and, as a result, have difficulty maintaining his mechanics and making consistent solid contact. He'll be looked upon as an "easy out."

Every hitter should know what his personal strike zone looks like and what it looks like from a pitcher's viewpoint. A hitter's strike zone should be drawn on a wall for visual awareness and practical purposes. Find a wall that is flush with the floor and is seen daily (bedroom, basement, garage, etc.). From your stance position, stand with your back foot against the wall, as if viewing a pitcher on the mound. With pencil or chalk, while still in your stance, mark a dot on the wall at the top of your back knee and another dot at the very bottom of your back armpit (chest). Stand back, and with a straight edge, draw a vertical line connecting the two dots. From the top and bottom of each line, draw horizontal lines 17 inches across, which is the width of home plate. Then connect the other vertical line. Then, in alignment with the bottom corners of your strike zone, use tape, chalk, or a moveable plate to create a home plate on the floor, near or against the wall. Next, using a cylinder approximately the size of a baseball, draw circles inside and outside your strike zone. Now, step back and view what your personal strike zone actually looks likes. For a mental picture and as a visual aid, every time you pass by your zone, look at it. When entering or leaving your room or going to your car, take a look.

However, if you want to practice hand direction, face the wall with your front foot near it. While taking your stance, check your plate coverage and then practice hand direction to a ball in a particular location inside or outside your zone. With just your bottom hand (no bat is necessary), gain hand direction and limited extension to a specific ball. You will realize as your front elbow hinges how easily your hands respond on a downward path to those balls within your zone or what it feels like when your hands reach outward, lift, or cut inward in response to pitches that are not strikes but outside your zone—away, inside, up, or down.

A hitter who has a mental awareness of his zone, knows where he wants the ball, and is consistently swinging at strikes as he works the count will increase the number of good pitches he will have to hit,

Personal wall strike zone: for proper plate coverage, hand direction, extension, and visual awareness, home plate is divided into three areas based on left-handed hitter.

maintain his mechanics, and assure himself of more solid contact. As noted, believing each pitch will be yours to hit is being offensive-minded. Mentally knowing where you want the ball and "locking in" to that area while visually recognizing a pitch will allow you to determine its location early and correctly respond.

As part of your offensive game plan, knowing what type of pitches a pitcher throws for strikes will also provide a basis of where to look for specific pitches within your strike zone. For example, a pitcher shows that he has four types of pitches: a fastball, a curveball that breaks over the top and down, a slider that is sharp and moves toward the outer half of the plate, and a changeup that sinks. However, during the game, his curveball and changeup are inconsistent (out of the strike zone), and he is able to throw only his fastball and slider for strikes. Although still learning the pitches' rotation, movement, and location, by process of elimination and before two strikes a hitter can discount the curveball and changeup and put them at the bottom of his priority pitch list, thus narrowing his pitch selection to fastball, slider, and their locations. By knowing a pitcher's most consistent pitch is his fastball, it should be a hitter's priority pitch and the pitch he should be geared to hit. However, while looking for a fastball, he can anticipate a pitcher's second consistent pitch (in this example, a slider) and by recognizing it early respond easier to that pitch; or, with two strikes, he can adjust his timing (down) to an off-speed pitch. Generally, it's easier to slow down the timing of a swing by being prepared for a fastball and adjusting downward to an off-speed pitch than to speed it up by being prepared for a slower pitch and adjusting up to a fastball. However, on any pitch, if a hitter sees it early, he is not fooled or taken by surprise; his instincts and aggressiveness should take over and he should hit the ball well.

To his advantage, a hitter who is offensive-minded, who is recognizing pitches early and effectively using his strike zone and game plan, will dictate to the pitcher, catcher, and umpire what he will or will not swing at during his plate appearances. A hitter who is looking for his pitch and believing that the next pitch will be his pitch to hit (while being good enough to lay off bad balls or pitches he has not anticipated) will have developed into an aggressive yet smart (disciplined) hitter. While hitting, he will force a pitcher to throw strikes and put additional pressure to "come to him" with pitches that he can handle, especially with runners in scoring position. Mechanically, a hitter will consistently "stay within himself" and maintain his setup, timing, and swing. As a result, a hitter's overall offensive production will increase.

Once he knows his strike zone and uses it as a guide, location and count hitting is the next progressive step for a hitter. It is based on his knowledge of his strike and contact zones and his ability to channel his aggression with pitches in those locations. Depending upon a pitcher's consistency (as previously noted), different game situations, and count variations, a hitter has many options he can implement within his zones. However, before thinking about those options, the hitter must learn a key to location hitting: dividing the plate and his strike and contact zones into thirds—middle, middle-out, and middle-in. To coincide with this application, a hitter should divide the playing field into thirds: middle, opposite field, and pull side of the diamond. Using field perspective as an initial guide to where he wants to hit the ball will help a hitter time his swing within his strike and contact zones. Successfully attacking these pitch locations and field areas will allow him to cover the plate more effectively while limiting a pitcher's advantage to exploit a weakness in a particular zone.

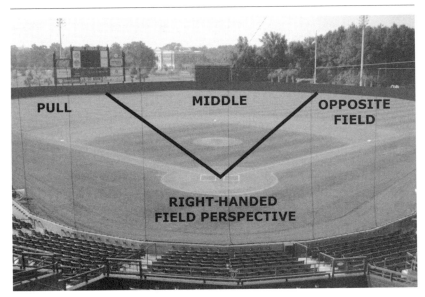

Right-handed field perspective

Because a hitter does not know a predetermined pitch location or what type of pitch a pitcher will throw, the most consistent approach a hitter can use, whatever the count situation may be, is to "think up the middle of the diamond," look for the ball out over the plate, believe the next pitch will be his, and then recognize and respond to the pitch. As noted, based on a fastball over the middle of the plate, if a hitter responds early so that his point of contact is ahead of his front foot, the ball will be hit to the pull side of the diamond. If contact is made in line with his front foot, the ball will be hit through the middle. If his response is late, but just behind his front foot, the ball will be hit to the opposite field. As initial guides, using middle locations of home plate as where to look for a pitch and the middle of the diamond for field perspective (left-center to right-center) as where to hit the ball will help a hitter stay with a pitch longer and more easily cover the outer half of the plate; yet in his response to a pitch on the inner half, he will still be quick enough to pull the ball. During all count situations, this type of mental game plan will help a hitter maintain his mechanics, points of contact, and overall offensive approach and should be implemented as part of his regular batting practice routine.

There are a number of other options available to a hitter in regard to location hitting. Depending on his circumstance, here are some examples:

- Location hitting based on dividing the plate in half. Before two strikes, a hitter may want to divide the plate and his zones in half and look all inside or outside, using primarily one side of the field or the other. By narrowing the plate, a hitter can effectively channel his aggression to a pitch within a set location where he is looking and that he wants to control. This approach can be helpful if a hitter is in a slump (although the first adjustment should be visual) or in a specific game situation where he is asked to move a runner, bunt a certain direction, or pull the ball. In this approach, it is advisable that if the pitch is not where a hitter is looking, he should lay off, be patient, and wait for a pitch in his zone—up to two strikes. However, for example, if his plan is to look for a pitch middle-in and pull the ball, yet he swings at a pitch on the outside corner, his timing and mechanics will suffer, as will his results.

- Location hitting based on strike count—no strikes, one strike, two strikes. Ball count is not important compared to the strike count. In this approach, a hitter's strike and contact zones expand as his strike count increases. For example, with no strikes (0-0, 1-0, 2-0, 3-0), a hitter can narrow his strike zone down and look for his pitch in the location he most desires. He can look "dead red." With one strike (0-1, 1-1, 2-1, 3-1), a hitter's strike zone, contact zone, and field perspective increase to middle pitch locations (middle-in to middle-out) and field areas (left-center to right-center gaps). The 3-1 count can be the exception and used as a "dead red" count; however, depending on a game situation (e.g., runners on second and third, first base open), a pitcher may not want to give in to a particular hitter and "groove one" but rather will throw a pitcher's pitch to induce weak contact or a missed attempt, knowing that if he eventually walks the hitter he can still have the double play in order. With two strikes (0-2, 1-2, 2-2, 3-2), a hitter's zones increase to their fullest extent as he looks to protect the entire plate. His pitch location should shift to middle-out, and his field perspective to the opposite field. In the two-strike count, a hitter should not be surprised by a fastball but should have learned enough during the count sequence to recognize an off-speed pitch, respond, and battle. In regard to the 3-2 count, a hitter should realize that a pitcher does not want to allow a walk but would rather have him hit to get on base and allow the chance for his defense to work for him. For that reason, often a hitter will get a better pitch to hit in this count than in the other two-strike counts.

- Location hitting based on count situations—ahead, even, or behind. A "hitter's count" is when he is ahead of the pitcher and the count favors him (0-0, 1-0, 2-0, 3-0, 3-1). In these counts, a hitter looks for his pitch and shifts his attention to where he wants a ball to hit solidly or "drive" (middle, middle-in). However, it should be understood that if the pitch is not where he is looking or a different pitch is thrown than what was anticipated, a hitter should lay off or risk the consequence of poor results (e.g., swinging at a marginal pitch and weak contact). Examples would be a right-handed hitter who is looking for a fastball on the inner half of the plate with left field in mind who becomes overly eager and swings at a pitch on the outer half or corner of the plate, or a hitter who is looking for a fastball but swings at a slider or changeup not in his location. Common results in both cases would be topped balls to the infield, lazy fly outs, or missed attempts. When a hitter is ahead in the count, the opportunity to succeed is in his favor and he should be locked in to his pitch and location, thus taking advantage of a pitcher's problem of being behind in the count. When a hitter is even in the count (1-1, 2-1, 3-2), he should shift his attention to middle locations (middle-out to middle-in) with middle-field perspective and respond to the pitch. Although the 3-2 count is an even count, it is a definite action situation for both hitter and pitcher. Having two strikes, a hitter should be mindful of covering the entire plate, recognizing early ball or strike, and responding correctly. However, if that pitch is too close to take (in, out, up, or down), swing! When a hitter is behind in the count (0-1, 0-2, 1-2, 2-2), he should shift his attention to middle-out with opposite-field perspective and, if needed, respond to pitches on the inner half. However, in these counts, if a hitter is too mindful of covering the outer half of the plate and looks too far away, a quick fastball on the inner half or inside corner of the plate may freeze his response and reaction time. As a result, a called third strike is common.

- Location hitting based on fewer than two strikes or with two strikes. In this approach, regardless of the count, with fewer than two strikes, a hitter narrows his pitch and location to what he most desires and stays within those perimeters, laying off pitches and locations that are not desirable. His field perspective is based on his pitch and location. With two strikes, a hitter increases his plate coverage to its fullest extent, uses the opposite field as perspective, and responds to any pitch that is too close to take.

Here are more helpful hints to location hitting and count situations. A hitter should realize that on a consistent basis, a pitcher will try to get ahead and stay ahead with his primary or most consistent pitch. Usually, that pitch is his fastball. Why? It is his most familiar pitch and one he is comfortable throwing. It is the easiest to control within the strike zone and the pitch he bases his mechanics on. If a pitcher has trouble during a game, his ability to command his fastball is a leading indicator. However, once in rhythm with this pitch, his others follow in order of consistency.

While growing up, playing baseball in the street, backyard, or Little League, the first pitch hitters learn to hit is a fastball. If a hitter fails in that, he never advances to the next level or he loses his desire to hit. It has been said that a reason hitters fail to move on and play higher levels is because they cannot hit a curveball. Here is a secret. A hitter at any level does not have consistent success by hitting good breaking balls. A hitter has success because he can hit a fastball while having the ability to recognize and lay off poor or even marginal off-speed pitches, especially up to two strikes. A question could be asked, "Does a hitter have success hitting breaking balls?" Yes; however, most are mistake pitches that are poorly located and up in a hitter's zone, or they are pitches he easily picks up from a pitcher's release point. A successful hitter thrives on fastballs. It is his learned pitch. It is a pitch that is constantly practiced to maintain mechanics, timing, and swing, and because it does not inherently change speeds or planes, a hitter can consistently judge it and more easily align his barrel on contact.

For those reasons, and because a pitcher attempts to get ahead and stay ahead with his most consistent pitch, a hitter should gear to hit his pitch (fastball) early and often in the count and hit it solid. As noted, early pitch recognition plays a key role, as does a hitter's ability to hit within his zones as he "works the count" while laying off bad pitches, especially up to two strikes. However, when a hitter is constantly behind (0-2, 1-2), he is often swinging early in the count at poor pitches, missing his pitch, taking it, or fouling off good pitches to hit. As a consequence, he has no choice but to widen his zones and routinely see more marginal strikes (pitcher's pitches) and off-speed pitches and have to battle for contact.

During early counts (0-0, 1-0, 0-1, 1-1), a hitter should stay ready for a pitcher's most consistent pitch (usually, his fastball), recognize early, and respond within his zones to his pitch with the intent of making solid contact ("don't miss it—hit it!"). During middle to late counts (2-1, 2-2, 1-2, 0-2, 3-2), a hitter should stay ready for a fastball but anticipate a pitcher's secondary pitch or "soft stuff" (curveball or changeup) depending upon the strike count.

Although two-strike hitting has been noted, its importance must be further discussed. Whether in a single game or over the course of a season, a hitter will face this strike count approximately 50 percent of the time. How effective he is in this count can make the difference between hitting .300 or .230. Make no mistake: two-strike hitting maximizes a hitter's instincts and stretches his true talent as an offensive threat.

There is no easy way to achieve success with two strikes. However, there are keys to having consistency in this area. A strong mental approach that provides confidence, courage, and a will to win can give a hitter an unseen advantage. Sound mechanics as well as consistent preparation and game plan will allow further advantages, as will knowledge of a pitcher (e.g., what is his "out-pitch," the pitch he commonly uses when he needs to put a hitter away or get an out, etc.), early recognition of pitch types, and the ability to use his zones and field perspective. All play significant roles for consistency while two-strike hitting.

Whenever the count moves to two strikes, a hitter does not have the luxury of looking for his pitch in his location, sitting "dead red," or thinking, "pull the ball." His priorities *must* change in regard to pitch selection, point of contact, and field perspective. To help maintain his mechanics and barrel coverage, and to "stay longer" with an off-speed pitch, a hitter should use an opposite-field or middle-of-the-diamond perspective as a guide to where he wants to hit, depending upon a pitcher's "stuff." A hitter must trust his ability to recognize pitch type and location early, and although he should not be surprised by a fastball, he should anticipate and adjust down to a pitcher's secondary or other off-speed pitches. He must realize his priority is to increase his plate coverage and zones to their fullest extent and swing at any pitch that is too close to take for a strike, thinking, "contact, contact, contact." In this two-strike situation, he must not give in emotionally by believing he is already doomed to fail because he either missed his pitch or swung at a bad pitch or because the umpire missed a call; instead, he must battle the pitcher's pitches as he continues to work the count and stay alive. With two strikes, a hitter needs to believe he can still hit the ball solidly, get a hit, put the ball in play making the defense work to get him out, or draw a walk. It takes one pitch to have success—that is why three strikes are given to a hitter, not two. Anything can happen, so stay confident, stay aggressive, and stay ready to respond.

As noted, a hitter should believe the next pitch will be his to hit regardless of his count situation; however, there are two counts that need to be addressed. Both are significant, and both can be used to a hitter's advantage: the 0-0 and 3-2 counts. Because the 0-0 count is the earliest count a hitter faces, weak contact is not an option. In this count, making poor contact with a marginal strike or on a pitch that is not anticipated or is outside a desired location will make a pitcher's job easy. In the 0-0 count, becoming an easy out is wasting a plate appearance and should be avoided. Because of those reasons, a hitter should address this count as being ahead and should "sit dead red." As in every plate appearance, early pitch recognition is a must, and for a hitter who is locked in, who is narrowing his zones to a desired location, and who is looking for a good pitch to hit, the 0-0 count will provide that opportunity and help him avoid chasing marginal stuff. Make no mistake, as in other hitter's counts, solid contact is expected and can be achieved when correctly approached.

The 3-2 count should be a count a hitter loves to hit in. As noted, early recognition is a must, but a hitter who is ready to swing at anything close (it is a two-strike count) and who also has the middle of the diamond as field perspective can take advantage of a pitcher's mind-set of "don't walk the hitter—make him hit to get on base" and can consistently get his primary pitch to hit. In this count, a hitter should believe that he will either swing with intent to hit a pitch solidly (line drive) or not swing because the pitch is ball four. In this count, it is also advisable for a hitter to stay in the batter's box until the umpire makes the ball-four call. He is there first to hit, then to take his base.

In all count situations, a hitter who has confidence in his ability and mechanics, who has a mental game plan that includes knowing what types of pitches a pitcher throws and how consistent he is with them for strikes, who knows his zones while using initial field perspective for guidance, and who recognizes pitches early for correct responses can consistently perform to his maximum potential.

20
Situational Hitting

Successful situational hitting can help a hitter and his team win without getting a hit, by correctly executing in game situations. Primary situations include these:

- Sacrifice bunting
- Hit and running
- Moving a runner over from second to third with no outs (with only second base occupied)
- Driving in a runner from third base with less than two out with a sacrifice fly, fielder's choice, or squeeze bunt

It should be noted that any time there is a hit with runners on base or in scoring position, "timely hitting" is the appropriate phrase and most desired result. However, a hitter who can advance runners 90 feet, either to score a run or put runners in scoring position without the use of a hit, will put added pressure on an opposing pitcher and defense while helping himself and his team win.

Hitting with a single purpose during a game situation can direct a hitter to look in a specific zone and hit (or bunt) to a specific side of the diamond to correctly accomplish the task even without getting a hit. Here are some examples:

- A hitter is asked to move a runner from second to third with no outs. For a right-hander, his job is to hit the ball, preferably on the ground, toward the opposite side of the diamond. His ability to recognize a pitch he can handle (middle to outer half of the plate), let the ball travel deeper in his contact zone, and hit the ball toward right field will do it. For a left-hander, his job is to pull the ball. Looking for a pitch he can turn on (middle to inner half of the plate) and hit early will advance the runner.

- With a runner at third base with less than two out and with the infield back, a routine fly ball or any ground ball not at the third baseman but toward the middle of the diamond past the pitcher will be rewarded. In the same situation but with the infield in, a hitter should be mindful of what a pitcher may do to incite a topped ground ball to his infield. Knowing that a hitter may be overly eager in this situation, he may throw his curveball or off-speed pitch to get the hitter off-balance and forward, inducing a weak ground-ball out. Before two strikes, a hitter should look for his pitch or a pitch in his location to drive. Solid contact is expected. In both of these game situations, a hitter should be mindful that trying to lift a ball to the outfield is not a sound mechanical swing and could put him in jeopardy of missed attempts, shallow fly balls, or pop-ups. In a situation that has runners on second and third with no out and the infield back (depending upon the manager's decision), a hitter may be asked to hit the ball on the ground to the opposite side of the diamond. If successful, he would have accomplished two things at once: driving a runner in from third while moving a runner over from second to third in the hopes that the next hitter can also drive a runner in from third, now with one out. In the same situation but with one out and the primary runner at third, depending upon the score and inning, the hitter should approach his plate appearance to get that runner in. Early recognition and dictation of his pitch selection and location will allow a hitter to "stay within himself" and get a good ball to hit, especially up to two strikes. With the bases loaded, the same approach is necessary to avoid chasing early or swinging at marginal strikes that may result in weak contact before the two-strike count.

While hitting with runners in scoring position with less than two out or with two out, a question needs to be asked: "Who is the pressure on—the pitcher or the hitter?" My answer would be, "The pitcher. He is the one who has struggled to put himself into this jam. He is the one who cannot afford to allow more base runners. He is the one having trouble locating his pitches, etc." As a hitter, regardless of the game situation, your overall mental approach should not change. This particular situation should be like any other as far as what you need to do: stay within your mental game plan and physical approach, control your emotions, and dictate to the pitcher, catcher, and umpire during your plate appearance. Relax, recognize, and respond to win.

Hitting with a purpose involves combining a hitter's mental and physical approach, his pregame preparations, and his ability to intensify his concentration and thought processes for the upcoming battle. A hitter who does this can, with confidence, compete with a clear purpose: to be an offensive threat and help his team win.

Although there is nothing spectacular about pregame preparation and practice, quality time spent here will pay off in spectacular game results. In the batting cage and during batting practice, a hitter should do the following:

- Fine-tune his mechanics with correct swing repetitions.
- Have any questions answered concerning his overall physical approach.

- Maintain rhythm and timing of swing to be as close to game-ready as possible.
- Maintain early recognition and visual awareness of pitches and their locations.

In the dugout, prior to a game and after his physical work, a hitter's final pregame preparation should begin:

- Mentally review the pitcher he will face and his types of pitches.
- Mentally go over the signs his manager has for game situations.
- If possible, watch the opposing pitcher warm up.

In the on-deck circle, a hitter should do the following:

- Watch a pitcher's delivery and how consistent he is with his release point and types of pitches.
- Pay attention to what the pitcher's secondary and out-pitch is as he works a hitter.
- Know the current situation and how that situation could change at any point (score, outs, runners on base, etc.). It could determine what the hitter may be asked to do, other than get a hit—e.g., bunt, hit-and-run, move a runner over from second, etc.
- If necessary, become a coach at home plate after a hit.
- Control emotions, breathe deeply, and relax.

In the batter's box is the time to take control of the situation. A hitter needs to do the following:

- Control emotions.
- Breathe.
- Intensify concentration.
- Channel aggression.
- Rely on a game plan.
- Relax, recognize, and respond.

Your purpose has been well defined, your preparation complete—now is the time for the battle to begin. Now is the time to win the battle!

21
The Hitter's Mental Practice Points

Review and encourage yourself on a regular basis. You are your best asset.

- Are you doubting or worrying about yourself? Trust your preparation and hitting ability no matter what the situation or end result.

- Are you tentative or defensive-minded? Be offensive-minded, be ready, and expect good things to happen. An aggressive, confident mental approach will prove that failure is not a threat.

- Are you overly anxious and out of control while hitting? Breathe! Relax, recognize, and then respond. Control your emotions rather than allowing your emotions to control you. During your plate appearances, be patient, resist panic, and then dictate your responses and actions. Do not allow the pitcher or any outside influences to change your positive mental approach or game plan.

- Are you locked up, having lost your focus and game plan? Lock in. Stay determined to accomplish your goals. Be consistent in your mental and physical preparation. Be open to instruction and willing to make adjustments when necessary.

- Are you isolating yourself? Whatever your personal circumstances may be, real leadership is seen during times of adversity. Have the will to lead others, in word and by example.

- Are you satisfied, and have you become complacent? Maintain a consistent mental and physical approach. Do not let up on yourself, but continue to strive to be the best you can be, every day and every game!

22
Hitting Drills

The following hitting drills are for the maintenance of a hitter's physical approach. They will help him develop muscle memory based on correct swing repetitions. They will reinforce correct use of his frontside and backside approach, timed with the combined effort of his lower and upper halves, encouraging balance, direction, quickness, and vision while maintaining correct swing extension, barrel angles, and points of contact.

Batting Tee

There are three main contact points and field directions. A batting tee set up in relation to a hitter's strike and contact zones will encourage the correct use of his mechanics, swing extension, and barrel coverage of home plate. A contact line is drawn inward from the spindle toward a hitter's batter's box as a guide for his front (stride) foot. Based upon the contact line and where his front foot lands in relation to it, the tee and ball location can be moved to a desired contact zone. This "dead ball" drill will also provide correct hand direction and barrel angle to the appropriate field area.

- **Middle-In Pitch Location.** A hitter's front foot falls behind the contact line. With correct hand direction and extension, a pull barrel angle should be achieved at point of contact and the ball hit to the pull side of the field.
- **Middle Pitch Location.** A hitter's front foot lands on the contact line or even with the batting tee's spindle. A center or flush barrel angle should be achieved and the ball hit up the middle of the diamond.
- **Middle-Out Pitch Location.** A hitter's front foot lands ahead of the contact line. Opposite-field barrel angle should be achieved and the ball hit toward the opposite field.

Soft-Toss Drills

In these drills, the ball is tossed from different directions to specific pitch locations.

- **"Regular" Soft Toss.** Instructor is at roughly a 45-degree angle to the hitter and flips the ball at a hitter's belt buckle, toward the center of the plate. Middle pitch locations should be the norm, with the center of the diamond used.
- **Side Soft Toss.** This is an extension of the batting tee drill. A hitter sees the ball from a side view, as all three points of

contact and field directions are used. The instructor is at roughly a 90-degree angle to the hitter in line with a hitter's front foot. For balls hit toward the opposite field, the instructor flips the ball behind the front foot. For balls hit toward the middle of the diamond, balls are flipped in line with the front foot. For balls hit toward the pull side of the diamond, balls are flipped ahead of the front foot. This drill will enforce "deeper" ball position (with ball movement) and help control a hitter's weight transfer as he maintains correct swing repetitions. Depending upon a hitter's needs, the instructor can move ball locations but must be mindful of a hitter's strike and contact zones, including his overall mechanics and the directional result of contact.

- **Frontside Soft Toss.** All three primary field directions and pitch locations are used. A batting practice screen is placed approximately 15 feet in front of and aligned with home plate. The instructor (from behind the screen) gives a firm toss from this front position to a hitter's primary pitch locations.
  - **Opposite field**—toss is toward outer half of plate. A hitter must allow the ball to travel deeper for correct barrel angle at contact. The correct result will be opposite-field contact.
  - **Center field**—toss is toward middle of plate. A hitter must allow the ball to travel for correct barrel angle at contact. The correct result will be contact toward center field.
  - **Pull field**—toss is toward inner half of plate. A hitter must recognize pitch location early, pivot quickly (to clear his front hip), and release his back hip, allowing his hands to gain extension and quickness during his swing. The correct result will be contact toward the pull field.

Optional Frontside Soft-Toss Drills

- **Hard/Soft Drill.** The instructor offers hard (firm) or soft (small to large arc) tosses. A hitter recognizes the difference between the two while maintaining his frontside and backside approach. The tosses can be alternated, mixed, or given in repeated order, depending upon a hitter's needs. The instructor flips the ball within a hitter's strike and contact zones, as the hitter recognizes and correctly responds.

- **Good-Ball/Bad-Ball Drill.** The instructor varies the tosses within or outside a hitter's strike and contact zones. The instructor can flip any variety of toss: hard, soft, good, bad, strike, or ball. A hitter recognizes strikes to hit or balls to lay off. He practices points of contact within his zones and locations as he correctly responds to what he sees. During this drill, a hitter's field perspective should be center-oriented; then, if required, he can respond to a ball on the inner half of the plate.

- **Out/In Drill.** The instructor tosses consecutive balls to outer or inner halves of the plate. A hitter establishes his points of contact (barrel angles) after consecutive tosses to each location, distinguishing (visually and physically) between those two primary locations. The instructor can alternate locations. If the instructor mixes locations (or hard to soft toss), the hitter's field perspective should be center-oriented, responding quicker to inner-half tosses.

- **Off-Center Soft Toss.** From a front position, the instructor moves the batting screen laterally toward a hitter's pull side and flips the ball across and away, simulating a pitch that "runs away" from the hitter toward the outer half of home plate. This drill will reinforce correct extension and deeper ball positions at contact while encouraging a hitter to wait and track a ball longer as he maintains his frontside and backside approach. Opposite- to middle-field perspective is used. If, during the drill, a hitter's point of contact is too early, he will have a pull barrel angle; common results will be topped ground balls to the pull side of the cage or diamond. Seeing and feeling the difference on contact, the hitter should make the necessary adjustments—mainly, letting the ball travel longer.

- **One-Hand Soft-Toss Drill.** A hitter swings with either his top or bottom hand to emphasize their specific functions. (Refer to Chapters 15 and 16 for review.) A hitter uses correct frontside setup and direction with backside deliverance of his swing, using primary points of contact. During swings, a hitter should feel the difference in strength between his front and bottom hand while maintaining their correct functions. Results of contact should be solid, and middle-field perspective should be the norm. For easy control of his hand action and barrel, a hitter can use a short bat or fungo, or he can choke up on his regular bat. All soft-toss drills can be used at the instructor's discretion, depending on a hitter's needs.

Short-Screen Batting Practice

This drill is really an extension of the frontside soft-toss drill. A batting screen is placed approximately 25 feet from home plate, a closer distance than during regular batting practice. The instructor throws overhand from this distance and should be able to maintain consistent pitch locations. He can throw consecutive pitches to the inner or outer half of the plate, alternate those locations, mix firm or soft pitches, or incorporate a good-ball/bad-ball drill, depending on a hitter's needs. A hitter should maintain his overall physical approach, strike and contact zones, field perspective, and early recognition of the pitch (flip his eyes from the instructor's head to his release), and he should follow the ball off his bat for good head position.

Pitching Machine Drills

Based on availability and type of machine, drills should be done from approximately 35 to 45 feet to help maintain pitch locations within a hitter's strike zone. Here are examples of drills and objectives for an instructor to use:

- **Game Situations Drill.** A hitter can practice sacrifice bunts, hit-and-runs, moving a runner from second to third with no outs, dealing with a runner at third with less than two outs (with infield in or back), dealing with bases loaded, etc. Repeating a specific situation can maintain a hitter's consistency. For example, the instructor can ask for five hit-and-runs in a row, and the hitter attempts to hit the ball on the ground five times.

Like correctly repeating swings, correctly repeating situations can build confidence to succeed.

- **Count/Location Situation Drill.** A hitter can use the different options as noted in Chapter 19. The instructor becomes umpire for all count situations. A hitter can start with the 0-0 count or begin with a count that is accelerated (1-1, 2-1). He works each count until the ball is put in play, and then he begins with a new one. These are location options a hitter can use during this drill:
  - Divide home plate in half, before two strikes. With two strikes, increase zones to cover the entire plate.
  - Narrow or widen zones and field perspectives, depending upon strike count.
  - Hit with fewer than two strikes (solid contact is the objective) or hit with two strikes (change field perspective to opposite field, maximize zones, and battle for contact).
  - Whatever the count, stay center-oriented and respond to a pitch middle-in.

  In all examples, field perspective should be used as an initial guide.
- **Solid-Contact Drill.** The goal is for a high percentage of solid contacts based on the amount of swings a hitter takes within a batting practice round. An example would be for a hitter (or hitters, if an instructor wants to make this drill more competitive) to receive 10 swings during his round. A ratio of 7 out of 10 would be considered good, or, during a game between hitters, the player with the highest number of solid contacts would win. Solid contacts are determined at the instructor's discretion. This drill should divert a hitter's thought processes from his mechanics to how solidly he can hit the ball—as it should be during a normal game plate appearance.
- **Right- and Left-Handed Breaking-Ball Drill** (if available). This is an extension of the off-center soft-toss drill. Use a right-handed breaking ball for right-handed hitters and a left-handed breaking ball for left-handed hitters. At a shortened distance of 35 to 45 feet, a breaking ball that rolls across or has a small slide

(middle-in to middle-out plate locations) rather than one that quickly cuts or has a big downward arc should be the norm to best accomplish this drill. This drill will reinforce deeper ball positions and swing extension within a hitter's contact zone and provide recognition and tracking of an off-speed pitch (mainly running away) while allowing the hitter to maintain his frontside and backside approach with the correct release of weight transfer and timing of his hands. A hitter should use center- to opposite-field perspective as his initial mental guide; however, if a pitch hangs up middle-in, he should respond accordingly. It should be noted that a right-handed hitter should also practice on left-handed breaking balls, and a left-hander should practice on right-handed breaking balls. In each case, a hitter should maintain his points of contact ("let the ball travel") and then correctly extend through the pitch or risk topping or rolling over it.

- **Dual Pitching Machine Drill** (if available). This drill requires two machines set on a large tripod. When operating from a distance of 45 feet, one machine is set to throw fastballs and the other, breaking balls. The instructor stands behind the tripod and holds up two balls to show a hitter; then he simultaneously lowers the balls and feeds either the fastball or breaking-ball machine. This drill will teach a hitter to stay ready to hit a fastball yet adjust his timing downward when he sees a breaking ball. It will discourage guessing what a pitch could be or where it might be, etc., while encouraging a hitter's confidence in recognizing pitch type and location as well as overall hitting ability. At the instructor's discretion, alternate pitches (hard to soft) or any ratio (three fastballs to one breaking ball, etc.) can be thrown. Depending upon a hitter's needs, game or count situations can also be practiced, or he may want to track the difference between the two speeds, working on his setup, load, etc.

Team Batting Practice

A consistent routine can be designed to incorporate a hitter's mental game plan and physical approach. There are many different versions of batting practice. The instructor will decide how many swings a hitter will receive and what situations to perform in each round. This example incorporates a warm-up round, situational round, and solid-contact rounds:

- First round: two bunts (one each direction) and five swings (line drives) through the middle of the diamond or opposite gap. This round is designed as a warm-up to reinforce deeper ball positions, field perspective, and points of contact while maintaining a hitter's frontside and backside approach.
- Second round: game situations (based on the instructor's discretion). Swings can include (in order) a hit-and-run, moving a runner over from second to third with no out, and scoring a runner at third with the infield in or back with less than two out. The instructor can have hitters take one swing for each situation or multiple swings for the same situation (five swings—five hit-and-runs, etc.) as a repetitive drill, discarding the other situations that day. A hitter can finish this round with three swings of two-strike hitting or hitting with fewer than two strikes. Incorporating a second round such as this would involve approximately eight swings.
- Third round: five swings. A hitter uses this round for solid contacts, maintaining his zones and field perspectives as guides.
- Fourth round: three swings. A hitter uses this round as a continuation of the third round.
- Fifth round: A hitter uses this round as a continuation of the fourth round but receives only two swings. However, if on his second swing he hits a line drive to the outfield grass (base hit), he remains hitting as a reward and is given an additional swing or swings depending on his final result.

When routinely implemented, this example of team batting practice, although approximately 23 swings, combines a full spectrum of offensive activity during a practice session and will provide purpose and consistent preparation for an upcoming game. However, for a hitter to maintain his swing and overall approach, it should be understood that more "free" swings (at the instructor's or a hitter's discretion) are necessary on a consistent basis, either in a batting cage or on the field.

No-Stride Drill

This drill incorporates balance while reinforcing frontside direction and setup with correct backside hip rotation and weight transfer for consistent timing and deliverance of the swing. To implement this drill, a hitter should do the following:

- Take his stance position.
- Take his stride back toward the pitcher's mound and, once landed (if needed), spread his feet at least the width of his shoulders.
- From this setup position, check for correct body weight distribution.
- Check for correct front-foot direction and frontside body alignment.
- From this setup position, place hands on hips and, without moving the front foot, pivot on the back foot to release back-hip rotation (front hip will respond and rotate naturally) and weight transfer to and against a firm inner frontside foot, thigh, and leg.
- At completion of drill, belt buckle should be facing the pitcher's mound.

A hitter should, slowly at first, repeat this action allowing his back foot to initiate the release and rotation of his back hip and weight transfer. As he accomplishes this action, he should quicken it while maintaining his balance. Next, he can do the No-Stride Drill using his bat and regular load and swinging. This drill can be used with a batting tee, other soft-toss drills, or regular batting practice. Some hitters have used this approach during games.

To incorporate this drill with normal swing action and use of the stride foot, all actions should be in rhythm and made once the front foot has landed. A hitter will quickly notice that if, during his stride, he has not set up correctly but pushed off his back foot, has lunged forward with his front foot, or has allowed his hands and hips to slide or glide forward with his front foot, his balance, backside rotation, and correct weight transfer will have all suffered the consequences. (Refer to Chapters 7 and 8.)

A hitter should practice with a purpose and for specific reasons. Whether those include correctly executing a game situation, narrowing or increasing his zones and field perspectives for better responses, maintaining his swing extension and quickness, or recognizing pitches early, the desire to be consistent and improve will elevate his ability and overall purpose.

Instructors should teach based on a hitter's needs. Using different drill options will accomplish this while also maintaining a hitter's mental and physical approaches. From batting tee and soft-toss drills to pitching machine drills and regular batting practice, all drills are designed to encourage and combine the positive mental and physical fundamentals within *Hit like a Big Leaguer*. A hitter who has correctly learned through instruction and experience and who is confident in his hitting ability can rise to his highest potential.

Hall of Famer Ted Williams, one of the greatest hitters of the past century and the last player to hit .400 (while maintaining great power numbers) was well ahead of his time. During his career he would analyze, dissect, and film his swing, trying to learn and gain whatever advantage he could while becoming a great hitter. He was a student of himself and his own best teacher. At the end of his illustrious career, he wrote his own book, *The Science of Hitting* (New York: Simon & Schuster, 1986), detailing his many thoughts. He stated, "My first rule of hitting was to get a good ball to hit." Simple, yet direct. Get a good ball to hit. Make no mistake: correct information is exceedingly valuable. While practicing, a hitter should be consistently thinking, feeling, analyzing, and digesting information to apply to his overall approach. During practice, the quality, not quantity, of swings is what matters. However, there can be no substitute for a hitter's confidence and ability to relax during a game situation so his rehearsed and true talents can carry over to his game plate appearances and be rewarded.

Hitting instincts, physical tools, and a personal desire to learn, compete, and achieve are all inherent factors that every serious hitter needs if he is going to hit like a big leaguer and have success now and in the future. It is my hope that you will continue to enjoy and learn about the game of baseball and, in particular, the fundamentals of hitting.

Index